THE MEDICAL LOOPHOLE

The Ultimate Guide to Medical-based Financial Aid

Copyright © 2017 by Jason White

All rights reserved. No part of the material protected by this copyright notice may be reproduced or utilized in any form, electronic or mechanical, including photocopying, recording, or by using any information storage and retrieval system, without written permission from the copyright owner except for brief quotations in a review.

Notice: The information in this book is true and complete to the best of our knowledge. It is offered without guarantee on the part of the author or publisher. The author and publisher disclaim all liability in connection with use of this book.

Philip Freeman, editor

David Moratto, cover and interior designer

www.medloophole.com

First edition.

Printed in the United States of America.

Library of Congress Control Number: 2017903636

ISBN: 10: 0-692-85212-3

ISBN: 13: 978-0-692-85212-5

THE MEDICAL LOOPHOLE

The Ultimate Guide to Medical-based Financial Aid

JASON WHITE

I dedicate The Medical Loophole *to each of the students and readers who will use its information to obtain financial assistance with college expenses. Student loan debt is the single biggest financial obstacle that students face today. So I consider it a personal victory each time a student qualifies for the medical-based scholarship program as a result of this book. I hope this book saves each of you a small fortune and allows you to move on with your life free of the burden of student loan debt.*

I also dedicate The Medical Loophole *to my wonderful family whose love and support means more to me than anything. Without you behind me, my success would mean nothing. I love all of you guys.*

A good teacher must know the rules;
a good pupil, the exceptions.
— Martin H. Fischer

There seems to be one quality of mind which seems
to be of special and extreme advantage in leading him
to make discoveries. It was the power of never
letting exceptions go unnoticed.
— Francis Darwin

CONTENTS

PREFACE	xi
1 INTRODUCTION	1
2 HOW DID I GET HERE?	5
3 ABOUT THIS PROGRAM	21
4 STARTING THE APPLICATION & DETERMINING YOUR ELIGIBILITY	31
5 GETTING PREPARED FOR YOUR FIRST MEETING	41
6 YOUR SECOND MEETING	49
7 REASONABLE ACCOMMODATIONS	57
8 CONCLUSION	63
APPENDIX A: DIRECTORY OF VOCATIONAL REHABILITATION OFFICES	69
APPENDIX B: SAMPLE LETTER TO YOUR DOCTOR	81
APPENDIX C: FREQUENTLY ASKED QUESTIONS	83
ABOUT THE AUTHOR	89

PREFACE

I was sitting at my desk in the Florida Attorney General's Office when a young woman appeared at my door. She had been speaking to one of the attorneys I worked with about going to college, and the subject of financial aid had come up. My coworker told her that I had received "some kind of scholarship based on asthma and allergies." She also suffered from asthma and allergies. So now she was at my office door, bristling with enthusiasm as she peppered me with questions about this medical-based scholarship program.

As always, I was willing to help a student who was struggling to figure out how to pay for college. I had been there myself, so I sympathized with her. I taught her everything I knew about the medical-based scholarship program that I had used to pay for college at East Tennessee State University. I helped her get the proper documentation needed to apply for the program, I helped her figure out where to submit her application, and I gave her tips on how to improve her chances of qualifying. I was pretty certain she would qualify if she would just go through the application process.

After a few weeks passed, I ran into her again in the hallway at work. As we made small talk, I asked her what was going on with her application for the medical-based scholarship program. For the last few weeks I had been fielding questions and helping her just about every day. It seemed like she should finally be ready to apply.

To my surprise, she told me she had changed her mind about applying for the medical-based scholarship program. She told me she had just signed up for a federal student loan, but not to worry — the interest rate was pretty good and it seemed like it was a lot easier than applying for the medical-based scholarship program. I couldn't believe what I was hearing. No matter how good a deal it was, it couldn't have been better than free money she didn't have to pay back!

I thought about her situation the rest of the afternoon. It began to irritate me that I had spent so much of my time and effort trying to help her, only to watch her face-plant straight into student loan hell at the last minute. This incident prompted me to start thinking about writing *The Medical Loophole*. I knew a book on this subject could potentially help lots of people who *really* wanted to be helped.

The Medical Loophole began to take shape as I did my best to recall and write down everything I had discussed with this young woman over those few weeks in my office. Eventually the notes from those conversations morphed into the book you are holding today. Until now, the information in these pages was largely available only by word of mouth. As far as I know, this book is the only one in the entire financial aid/college prep genre that specifically addresses this wonderful program. I am excited to know it is now available to anyone who is willing to pick up a book and read about it. I sincerely hope this book helps you achieve your wildest dreams.

～ 1 ～
INTRODUCTION

Congratulations! You have just discovered the world's best-kept financial aid secret! Unfortunately, most students never learn about the exciting possibility of paying for college on the basis of their medical condition. However, the federal medical-based scholarship program I'm going to teach you about covers many common medical conditions, such as allergies, asthma, ADHD, anxiety, and depression — just to name a few. Millions of students suffer from these everyday medical conditions, and therefore potentially qualify for the medical-based scholarship program. But only a small fraction of that number ever takes advantage of this program to pay for college expenses. The sad reality is, most students (about 12 million each year) will take out student loans to pay for college. And on average, these students will each rack up over $30,000 in student loan debt before they graduate. However, many of these students undoubtedly have some medical condition that could have helped them qualify for financial assistance and avoid the burden of student loan debt.

According to Families USA, approximately 20 percent of people aged 18–24 suffer from some type of significant medical condition. This means that out of the 12 million students each year who apply for student loans, more than two million of them may have qualified for financial assistance to pay for college on the basis of their medical conditions. This in turn means that, collectively, these millions of students may unnecessarily borrow around $70 billion dollars over the course of their time in college. The scope of this financial tragedy is nothing short of epic when you realize that this is roughly equivalent to the gross domestic product of Paraguay! All that money down the drain and gone forever simply because students failed to take advantage of a financial assistance program that they probably qualified for.

So how many students are actually taking advantage of their medical conditions in order to pay for college? Only around 100,000 students in any given year use the federal medical-based scholarship program I'm going to teach you about. This number fluctuates slightly from year to year, but generally speaking, this is a good estimate of national participation in any given year.

But why don't more students take advantage of this program? The simple fact of the matter is, most students never learn about this program, so it's impossible for them to take advantage of it. My goal is to dramatically alter this state of affairs. This program deserves to be front-page news. Every student who potentially qualifies for this program should be aware of it and know how to apply. There's nothing worse than borrowing money that you could have gotten for free.

Each year, the student loan industry rakes in billions of dollars from people just like you. And to protect their profits, this industry has successfully lobbied Congress for a law that makes student loan debt non-dischargeable even in bankruptcy. Gambling debts are dischargeable in bankruptcy! But student loan debt — not so much. Essentially, if not paid, student loan debt will follow you to the grave. My goal is to help you avoid becoming a victim of the student loan bullies by helping you capitalize on something you already have: your medical condition.

The medical-based scholarship program I'm going to teach you about personally saved me approximately $96,000 in student loan debt. I'm a true believer in this program, because I've seen it work time and time again. I know this program has the potential to work for you, because I've helped so many people just like you take advantage of it. In the following pages, I can confidently give you the benefit of my experience with the medical-based scholarship program, because my undergraduate degree was completely funded in this way and my law school degree was partially funded in this way. As I walk you through the simple application process for this wonderful program, I'm going to give you tips on how to improve your chances of qualifying and tell you everything you need to know to make this program work for you. But at the end of the day, only *you* can make it happen. As you learn about the medical-based scholarship program, commit yourself to a course of action. With the right information and a little effort on your part, you might be as grateful as I am that I learned about this incredible program.

I realize a lot of parents may be reading this book to help their children find ways to pay for college. So I have included a section at the end of each chapter just for you. I hope these sections address concerns that you might have. Taking an active role in helping your child embark upon this important journey is one of the most important things you can do as a parent. Your attention and participation in the process may help your child avoid serious financial mistakes. By learning about the medical-based scholarship program and assisting your child with the application process, you are leading by example and teaching your child what it takes to make good financial decisions.

I also expect that many students will be reading this book to find ways to pay for college expenses. If you are a student who is taking the initiative on your own to read this book, I sincerely applaud your determination. As the late great Billie Holiday once sang, "God bless the child that can hold his own." By picking up this book, you have already passed the first test of your college experience. You have decided to educate yourself without waiting for someone else to do it for you.

Many students I help out have never heard of this program, so they think it sounds too good to be true. Some simply can't comprehend getting free money for college on the basis of a non-debilitating medical condition like pollen allergies or ADHD. Students often ask me questions like, "Is this legal? Is this a real program? Why have I never heard of this?" In this book, I will give you the same answers that I give the students I help face to face. This book isn't about pulling a fast one on the system, lying, cheating, or trying to get something you don't deserve. It's about empowering you with the information that you need to get the maximum amount of financial assistance you're entitled to *under the law*. Everything I'm about to share with you is 100 percent legal and follows the letter of the law to a T. The government agency that runs the medical-based scholarship program approves applicants when they tell the truth, even if that truth is that their only medical problem is something simple like allergies. In the pages that follow, I'll explain why students have never heard of this program, and I will prove to you that it is *not* too good to be true.

Parent's Corner

Whether you realize it or not, you've been paying for the medical-based scholarship program your entire working life. Each year, when you pay federal income taxes, some of that money goes to fund the program I'm going to teach you about. Essentially, you've been footing the bill for a long time for someone else's kid to go to college on the basis of their medical condition. Therefore, you shouldn't feel embarrassed, guilty, or ashamed about asking for some of your own money back, now that you need it for your soon-to-be college student. The IRS accepts money from you and other taxpayers because that's what they are entitled to under the law. You too should get the money you're entitled to under the law. I am going to teach you how.

~ 2 ~

HOW DID I GET HERE?

It was Friday night, senior year, and I had just finished watching my high school's homecoming football game. As me and six or eight of my closest friends piled into my 1990 Honda Civic hatchback, we were deciding where to go next.

"I hear Jeff's having a bonfire in the field behind his parent's house," said Chris.

"Let's go play guitar at John's house," Will offered.

"I hear Brandon's parents are out of town, and he's throwing a party," replied Aaron.

Any time one of my friends uttered the words "parents out of town," there was an instant shift in the focus of our conversation. "Parents out of town" meant something significant. It meant an opportunity to experience unsupervised, belt-fed, fully automatic, teenage social interaction—the dangerous stuff. The stuff they warn you about in cheesy health education videos and public service announcements, the kind where at the conclusion of the story, the main character is pregnant, addicted, arrested or all of the above. We knew bad choices, minus parents, equals good story. So of course, Brandon's house was where we went!

As we pulled up, we discovered roughly one hundred of our classmates had made the same questionable choice that evening, as evidenced by the long line of cars stretched around the block. Once we found a place to park, we walked down the street, eagerly anticipating whatever carnage might lie ahead. As we got closer, we began to see the faint glint of commotion outside Brandon's house. Upon arrival, we discovered that a group of our most esteemed classmates had procured a couple of shopping carts to assist with the evening's entertainment of improvised bobsled races. Brandon lived just around the corner from a grocery store, so it wasn't hard to imagine someone borrowing a couple of carts for some innocent fun.

Inside, the house was smoky, loud, and crowded with teenagers who couldn't seem to get a word in sideways. In the hallway, a gaggle of girls was consoling another, who was crying over a guy named Bobby. In the kitchen, an arm wrestling match was reaching a fever pitch, with profane outbursts of encouragement coming from the bystanders. In the bathroom, there were beer cans in the toilet and blood in the sink — probably the result of an earlier shopping cart crash. The walls rattled to the beat of loud '90s hip-hop. There were cigarette butts and more empty beer cans covering every available surface. I felt a little bad for Brandon. I knew he would need the help of an entire hazardous waste response team to clean up the place after everyone left. Even if he was fortunate enough to get it all cleaned up, a serious parental interrogation was sure to follow, as reports of the evening would invariably begin to trickle out.

After a few hours of this race to the bottom, I called it quits and began to collect my friends for the ride home. By the time I got everyone rounded up and dropped off, it was close to 2:00 AM. I made the turn onto my street and turned down the radio as I approached my house. I killed the engine and headlights as I coasted into the driveway. If I was quiet enough, maybe I could fool my parents into thinking I'd gotten home an hour earlier. I tiptoed through the house and got ready for bed. As I lay there, I reflected on the evening with a few laughs, and then it was lights out.

The next morning came all too soon, as I was launched into painful sobriety by my persistent alarm clock. I felt like I had only been asleep for an hour before it started spewing its message of hate. I backhanded the snooze button like it owed me money and went straight back to sleep. I repeated this assault on the innocent clock three or four more times before it finally *hit* me why my alarm clock was set for Saturday morning.

I instantly panicked! Today was a big day, and I was already late! There's nothing worse than abruptly waking up to the realization that you were already supposed to be somewhere else. I scrambled out of bed, fumbling to put on last night's smoky, stale clothes that were still conveniently laid out on my floor like chalk-outlined evidence from last night's crime scene. Within a few minutes of my desperate awakening, I was zipping down the road at an incredible speed to take the test that would determine whether I would be attending college after high school.

The silent focus of the students in the test room instantly confirmed my fears as I burst through the door. The test had already begun and I was just now arriving. Would they even let me sit for the exam? Was I going to have to delay college by one semester? What would my parents think? I didn't have time to think about all the downstream consequences of missing this exam as I pleaded my case to the test proctor while still trying to catch my breath. Fortunately, he let me take a seat and begin, and I quickly tried to make up lost time.

Head throbbing in unison with each heartbeat, I tried hard to calm my nerves and focus on the task at hand. I began reading the instructions for completing the first section of the test, my eyes rapidly darting back and forth as I tried to skim the instructions for the important stuff. I had finished about half of the questions in the first section when the test proctor cried, "One minute remaining." It was time for Operation Christmas Tree. I say Christmas tree because that's the shape the black marks seemed to create as I spread out my guesses down the multiple-choice answer sheet. As I filled in the last circle, the test proctor yelled, "Time's up, pencils down."

I was a little frustrated that I didn't get a chance to read the remaining questions in the first section, but I was more relieved that the first section was over. The end of the first section provided me a brief opportunity to unwind from the panic mode I'd been in since my rude awakening. It gave me a chance to relax and get my mojo straight before the next section began.

Not Exactly Scholarship Material

A student with higher aspirations might not have recovered so gracefully from the morning's turbulent beginning, but I wasn't there to set any records. As you might have guessed, I was not exactly a model student in high school — in terms of behavior or grades. In fact, during most of my high school years, I was somewhere between a B and C student, and that suited me just fine. I honestly can't recall ever doing more than 30 minutes of studying on any given day all through high school. I suspected that one day, no one would care about my high school grades, or whether I had played a sport or joined a club. The only thing they would care about was the fact that I had graduated and gotten into college. If I could effortlessly cruise my way to a B or a C, that simply meant my time was freed up to pursue more interesting things. For better or worse, I saw high school merely as a low-level hoop one had to jump through to get to the next phase of life.

I was pretty sure I didn't need to ace the SAT that day in order to succeed in life. Looking back, I wish I hadn't cut it so close, but ultimately, scoring a few points higher on that first section really would have made no difference in my life's outcome. I wasn't interested in attending an Ivy League college, I had no illusions of saving the world through a perfect SAT score, and all I really wanted was to score high enough to get into East Tennessee State University, the local school where many of my friends were headed. Lucky for me, when my SAT scores came back, it turned out I had accomplished that goal. At that point, I certainly didn't regret going to the homecoming party and being a little late for the SAT the next day! The way I saw it, I had scored an A+ in Fun at the expense of a C+ in Responsibility. This was an acceptable tradeoff for me at that point in my life.

College Begins

After surviving my near-death experience with the SAT, the last few months of high school rapidly came to a close. I managed to graduate, to the surprise of many. I was accepted into East Tennessee State University and set about the task of picking a major. The whole concept of majoring in something was foreign to me. In high school, I just took whatever class they put me in. Now, I had some degree of choice to exercise, and I wasn't at all sure what to do with it.

In 1998, when I entered college, computer science was one of the hottest career paths in the country. The Internet Age had just begun to take off. Regular people were finally able to afford things like cell phones and personal computers. It was an unusual period of transformation for my generation. We were the last kids to grow up without the Internet, but we were still young enough to embrace it as our own when it arrived.

This era brought interesting change for everyone. It would be three years before most people would even hear of text messaging, and six years before Facebook would be invented. It was the middle of the "dot-com bubble," as it came to be known, and there was a palpable frenzy around anything having to do with computers. A modern industrial revolution had blasted off in Silicon Valley, and everyone wanted a piece of the action. So after much discussion, my family and I concluded that I should throw in my lot with this new technological trend and major in computer science when college began that fall.

While I wasn't exactly interested in computers, I thought computer science was a great career path to take. It felt like I was making a very grown-up decision about my future. I started researching computer science jobs and was pleased to learn they paid really well right out of school. In fact, I think it was the highest-paying major for undergraduates that year. My interest was further stoked by media reports of companies offering new BMWs to recent computer science graduates to come work for them. I became excited about my decision to major in computer science even though I didn't really know much about it. It was something new and different, and in time, I was sure I would learn to love it.

The Storm Clouds Gather

I was only a few weeks into my new major before I started getting hints of trouble. The concepts being presented in my computer classes were very abstract, and I was having difficulty making real world connections to the study material. I spent long hours at the university's computer lab, trying to make sense of computer programs that I really didn't understand. Sometimes I would arrive at the lab at the same time as other students in my classes. I knew we were working on the same assignment, but I was there for hours and they were gone in minutes. It was a clear sign to me that something wasn't clicking on my end. For the first time in my academic career, I felt outgunned.

Knowing that I had never really tried very hard in school, I decided the problem was that I wasn't working hard enough. I began to question the study habits I had developed — or failed to develop — in high school. I concluded that I had never really learned to work hard for my grades, and that if I wanted to succeed in college I would have to change this. So I committed myself to putting in as much time and effort as it took to succeed. After all, I had always heard that if you work hard you could be anything you wanted.

After a rough first semester, I anxiously awaited my report card. I was nervous about my grades, because I knew they weren't going to be stellar, but then again, they never had been before. But I wanted to get the shock over with and begin the winter break. When my report card arrived, I mentally prepared myself to pull off the Band-Aid. I knew I was cutting it close but had hopes that my determined efforts to succeed would pay off. And as it turns out, they did pay off — well, sort of. I somehow managed to narrowly pass all of my computer science classes. All was not lost. I had a glimmer of hope. I had never worked so hard in my life for such low grades, but at the end of the day, I had met the bare minimum requirements. I hoped the next semester would be much smoother. I was optimistic that I had made the necessary changes to my study habits and things would get better.

The Concrete Begins to Dry

As the second semester began, I tried to retain each piece of information like it was going to one day save the world from a nuclear Armageddon. I never missed a class, I was always prepared, I studied and worked hard, and my days became ever more centered on my studies. I felt like I was at the top of my game. I was giving it my best shot, and hated the thought of losing. In high school, I had been the kid who got a B without opening a textbook. In college, I was working incredibly hard just hoping that I could be average.

Despite my best efforts, I was still struggling as the second semester's exams got underway. The problem was easy to understand: My second semester's classes built upon the skills I was supposed to have mastered in the first semester's classes. But I had barely scraped by in those classes, and utterly failed to master anything. In fact, I could have probably retaken all those first-semester classes and not fared much better the second time around. I knew I was in serious trouble, but the only solution I saw was to redouble my efforts and dedicate even more time and energy to my studies. So, my strategy was to keep trying the same thing in the hope that my hard work would eventually overcome my lack of talent.

But there were only so many hours in a day I could spend studying. For every hour of class, I spent many more hours studying and doing homework. Life was no longer fun, and I was seriously stressed for the first time in my life. I felt like I was walking in wet concrete that was rapidly drying around me, each step requiring more effort than the last. My confidence started to take a nosedive as each new assignment arrived like another bloodletting. My stomach churned with anxiety at the beginning of each class.

As the second semester came to an end, I knew I had fared much worse than I had the semester before. I'll never forget the disappointment of scoring 17 points out of 100 on an exam that I had studied particularly hard for. The rest of the exams in my computer classes were similarly atrocious. It was clear I was facing checkmate. I had failed almost all of the classes in my major. I was now on formal academic probation. Something had to change.

Syntax Error

As the summer break began, I prepared to conduct an autopsy on my computer science career. I didn't learn very much about computer science during those two semesters. In fact, I still struggle with basic computer stuff to this day. But it was not a total loss. I learned a lot about myself, even in the face of stark failure.

I learned for the first time that I was capable of incredible feats of ambition when I really wanted something. I had never worked so hard toward a goal in my life. In the end, I failed despite all that effort, but I was proud of myself for how hard I tried to make it work.

I also learned that tremendous effort isn't a substitute for a complete lack of natural talent. It didn't matter how hard I worked at a subject I was no good at. It would never be enough to succeed, let alone compete with students who had a real aptitude for computers on their side. It became clear to me that I needed to capitalize on my strengths rather than trying to compensate for my weaknesses.

But the lessons didn't end there. I also learned that when someone financially invests in your future, it's important to instill them with confidence in your abilities. My parents' financial confidence in my academic abilities had effectively reached its end. They decided they would no longer pay my tuition, due to their legitimate concerns that college wasn't my thing.

It was completely my fault. I had given them all the reasons they needed to arrive at this conclusion. I had always been incredibly average in school, I'd had some minor teenage behavior issues, and I had just bombed my first two semesters of college. It looked from the outside like I had finally hit an academic wall that I had been speeding toward for years. I couldn't blame them for their decision at all. It made perfect sense.

With my academic future in a tailspin, every day at my pizza delivery job began to feel like the first day of the rest of my life. It was no longer a fun college job that I would eventually leave for something better — it was now my "career." I had cartoonish visions of myself at age 40, driving a noisy old car that reeked of stale pizza and broken dreams. I envisioned myself bitterly making deliveries to my old college dormitories and getting no tips. I began to see my pizza uniform as a symbol of unfulfilled ambition, a testament to my failed attempts at something better. To this day, I still can't stand to wear the color red.

As I dissected the problems I encountered during those two semesters, I eventually came to the conclusion that I had to do two things to turn my situation around: First, I had to choose a new major that I had natural talent for. I had learned there wasn't enough hard work in the world to compensate for a complete lack of natural talent. To stand a chance, I had to pick something I was good at. Second, I had to find a way to pay for college that didn't involve my parents writing a check. Even though they eventually agreed to keep funding my attempts at college, it weighed on me that I was putting them at risk financially. My confidence had taken a hit when I failed out of computer science, and I was worried I might suffer a similar fate even in a new major. So I really needed to find some way to pay for college on my own. At least then if I failed again, the consequences would land squarely on me and no one else.

Figuring out how to choose a new major, one that I had talent for, was the easy part. I looked at my grades from the previous two semesters and noticed something that hit me like a ton of bricks. I had failed my computer science classes even though I had worked incredibly hard and spent all my time on them. However, I'd gotten B's in English and political science. These two classes were shining beacons of light emanating from the black holes of my first two report cards. I had done nothing more than show up for these two classes and take notes while I was there. That's all the effort I could afford to expend, because I had been too busy trying to keep my other classes from going over the cliff.

What would happen if I had put as much time and effort into these classes as I put into the ones I had failed? I became certain that I could have easily gotten A's in those two subjects with just a little more effort. So I decided it made sense to become an English major with a minor in pre-law.

How to Pay For It?

Certain that I had found a major I had some talent for, the next step was to find a way to pay for my education. I began researching scholarships, grants, work studies, and any other thing I could think of that could potentially help me pay for college without taking out student loans. I was still somewhat nervous about failing out of school despite a change in major, so I really wanted to avoid student loans if at all possible. In the worst-case scenario, I would have to repay my student loans on a pizza delivery man's salary. This was a frightening possibility I wanted to avoid.

After a few weeks of educating myself in the subject of college financial aid, I stumbled upon an obscure government program that piqued my interest. It was created in 1973 and appeared to provide money for college on the basis of a student's medical condition. On its face, this program seemed to meet all my requirements. Unlike merit-based scholarships, it didn't require perfect grades, it didn't consider extracurricular activities, and it didn't require writing any essays. Unlike need-based scholarships, it wasn't entirely based on my family's financial situation.

I began to see this program as a potential solution to my college funding problem. The only question was whether my medical conditions, asthma and allergies, would qualify. I had my doubts about this part. While my medical conditions were certainly unpleasant, I just didn't see them as being serious enough to qualify. When I thought about medical-based scholarship programs, I thought of people confined to wheelchairs. To all outward appearances, I looked completely handsome and healthy. Well, healthy at least. I imagined my application landing in the office, and a government clerk instantly doubling over with laughter right before red-stamping it "DENIED." But as I read more and more about this government program, I couldn't find anything that appeared to outright disqualify me based on my particular medical conditions. So I decided to take the leap and submit an application. I wasn't about to let something I potentially qualified for slip through my fingers. Especially when it was money I didn't have to pay back!

The application was pretty straightforward — a few standard forms that asked for all my personal information, including a few questions about my medical conditions. The instructions said to complete the forms, mail them to the address listed at the bottom of the page, and that someone would contact me when the application was reviewed. As I watched the application drop into the big blue mailbox and the door slammed with a thud, I crossed my fingers.

After I submitted the application, a few weeks passed without any news. The whole thing began to slip from memory as I went back to life as usual. I was still grappling with my college funding problem and exploring other options when one day, as I was about to deliver a pizza at work, my phone rang. The voice on the other end asked to speak with Mr. White. No one ever called me Mr. White. What was going on here?

"Yes, this is he," I cautiously replied. The voice asked if I had recently applied for a medical-based scholarship program.

My heart leapt as I fumbled for my response. "Uh, yeah, I did apply for that program."

The voice asked if I was available for a short personal interview later in the week. *You bet your ass I was available for a short personal interview later in the week!*

As the call ended, I was so ecstatic I almost forgot I had a pizza to deliver. The fact that I had received a call was confirmation that things were happening! My application had at least been looked at. The voice on the phone didn't tell me I had qualified, so in hindsight I don't know why this news put such a spring in my step. But it felt like I had a real chance! My thoughts quickly turned to this personal interview I had agreed to come in for. What did they want to talk about? The rest of the week crawled by as I anticipated my appointment and the potential topic of the personal interview.

On the day of the appointment, I arrived about 30 minutes early. I was sitting in the parking lot of a government office that didn't appear to have any affiliation with the college campus a few miles away. The sign on the building said "Department of Human Services." I thought I'd gone to the wrong address because it sounded like a place you'd go to sign up for unemployment benefits, not a place where you applied for a scholarship program.

I entered the lobby, and the receptionist confirmed my appointment. That meant I was in the right place, but I was still somewhat confused. The waiting room was full of people from all walks of life. I was expecting a room full of college-age students, but that was not the case. A few minutes passed, and eventually my name was called. A middle aged lady in a jean skirt escorted me back through a maze of small cubicles. As we arrived at one of the middle cubicles, she said, "This is Steven, he will be taking care of you today."

Steven introduced himself and told me to have a seat. As we began to make our introductions, I noticed a small wooden sign on the edge of his desk that said, "Vocational Rehabilitation Counselor." I was confused by this title because it sounded like someone you'd talk to for addiction treatment. But my confusion began to clear up as Steven began speaking familiar words about the program I had applied for.

Steven seemed like a laid-back guy, and his polite demeanor made me feel like he was genuinely interested in getting to know who I was. I looked around his cubicle for additional clues about who he was. His desk was adorned with pictures of his wife and kids and some sports memorabilia. With his southern drawl and regular-guy interests, I felt like he was probably a guy I could easily relate to.

As the meeting got underway, Steven began filling me in on the details of the program I had applied for. Some of it was confusing. He kept saying the program was an "employment program." But I wasn't seeking employment — I needed money for college. But this fog soon cleared when Steven explained that paying for students to attend college helps to ensure those students become employed when they graduate. That was a good enough explanation for me. I had just spent the last few months thinking I would be employed as a pizza delivery driver my whole life. Any "employment program" had to beat that.

The meeting with Steven only lasted about 20 minutes. He asked me some questions about my medical conditions, like how the symptoms affected me, whether there were any jobs I felt I couldn't do because of them, and whether I was taking medication to treat them. We also discussed my education and career goals. I told Steven that I had originally been a computer science major and that it hadn't worked out very well. I told him I had decided I wanted to be an English major instead, and that one day I might consider going to law school. Steven requested that I bring my high school and college transcripts to our next meeting. He also wanted me to provide a copy of my medical records and tax records.

As we were ending our first meeting, Steven said something that made my day. He said, "I still need to review your medical records, but based on everything you've told me so far, you qualify for the program."

What? I had never tried so hard to conceal my excitement in my life! For some reason, I was worried an exuberant outburst would make it all disappear. But on the inside, I was exploding with joy and could have hugged this man I barely knew! I managed to keep the geyser contained until I could properly end the meeting. But when I finally got back to my car, it was time for a full-scale celebration. What a day! The smell of stale pizza and broken dreams had just been replaced by the sweet smell of success! I couldn't wait to share the news. It felt like my plan had come full circle. I instantly felt the stress of the previous year begin to melt away. It felt like I had been given a second chance and I already knew I was going to make the most of it. What a wonderful feeling.

At my next appointment with Steven, I brought him the transcripts, tax records, and medical records he'd requested. We then got down to the nuts and bolts of what the rest of my college experience would look like. We began filling out various forms and documenting my plan to major in English and minor in pre-law. To my surprise, the scholarship not only paid for all of my tuition and books, but also paid for some of my incidentals like gas and campus meals. This meant I did not have to worry about student loans or putting my parents at financial risk! I couldn't believe all the benefits of qualifying for this program!

Although it did come with some minor strings attached, they weren't anything I couldn't live with. Steven made me sign a document saying that in exchange for the money, I would take at least 12 credit hours each semester and I would maintain at least a C average. No problem! I was usually a C student anyway! After that, I was on my way back to college!

A New Leaf

When the fall semester began, an air of relief permeated my first day back. As I walked across campus, the university looked brighter, sounded sweeter, and had an aura of hope.

As I walked past the computer science building, a sudden jolt of mixed feelings came rushing back to me. I began to think about all the suffering and self-doubt I had endured in the computer science building.

I thought of all the blows my self-confidence had suffered, all the late nights I'd spent spinning my wheels on things I would never comprehend, and all the uncertainty about my future I had endured. But then I began to think about the deep new level of ambition I had discovered within myself in the computer science building. I thought about all the perseverance and determination I had discovered within myself in that building. All the grit and hard work I was capable of came flooding back to me in that moment. It was in that moment that I realized I had turned over a new leaf in my education strategy.

Effortlessly cruising my way to a B or C like I did in high school was no longer an option, even if I had enough natural talent for my new classes to allow for it. The genie was out of the bottle, and now there was no going back. I had discovered that I was capable of working hard for my grades and nothing less would suffice from here on out. For the first time in my life, I became an A student.

My stomach no longer churned at the beginning of class. Long gone were the days of eight-hour cram sessions followed by an academic bloodbath. My hard work now paid off with real results. Capitalizing on my natural talents while also dedicating myself to hard work turned out to be a powerful combination. It also led to another strange phenomenon: I actually began to enjoy learning for learning's sake. This is what I was supposed to be getting out of my college experience all along—not just a piece of paper at the end. It was the experience, the learning, the interaction, and all the immeasurable joys that come with finding out what you are good at. These were the things that mattered. The piece of paper at the end was just a formality.

Parent's Corner

"But I don't know what I want to be when I grow up." Does this line from your child sound familiar? Many students have difficulty deciding on a college major. With the pressure to get good grades in every subject, it can be difficult to determine your child's areas of natural talent. But discovering areas of

natural talent is incredibly important to success in college. Often times, the subjects of study that require the least amount of effort for your child are indicators of natural talent. However, these subjects can be easily overlooked as potential career choices or college majors because your child may consider these subjects boring or too easy. But your child may have so much natural talent for these subjects that he or she is simply not challenged or engaged by the lower level introductory classes. Have discussions with your child about potential career paths that build upon the subjects of academic study that require the least amount of effort for your child. This may help your child when deciding on a college major.

~ 3 ~

ABOUT THIS PROGRAM

Any discussion of the medical-based scholarship program needs to start with an understanding of where it came from. But first, I must address an intentional discrepancy I created regarding the name of the program. As you might have guessed, the official title of the program is "Vocational Rehabilitation Services." However, you might have also noticed that I call it the "Medical-based Scholarship Program." So why would I intentionally muddy the waters by calling this program by two different names?

One of the reasons so few students learn about this program is because its official title is not intuitive. The real name of this program (Vocational Rehabilitation Services) does nothing to convey to students what this program is about, and gives no clue as to who might qualify.

I didn't want to write a book that repeated this same mistake.

This program has been called "Vocational Rehabilitation Services" for nearly half a century, and the majority of students who might qualify for it still have no idea it exists. So when I decided to write this book, I quickly determined that a name change was long overdue. I hope that by calling this program the "Medical-based Scholarship Program," it will finally create awareness and increase participation by students who potentially qualify. But just note that I use both terms interchangeably.

Intuitive titles are incredibly important. There is nothing worse than hearing about someone in extreme student loan debt who would have clearly qualified for the medical-based scholarship program but never learned about it.

I recently met a young woman I'll call Laurie. Laurie was struggling to repay her student loan debt nearly 10 years after graduating. She had accumulated close to $200,000 in debt pursuing her professional degree, and still had over $150,000 left to repay.

Laurie clearly had a musculoskeletal disorder. When I told her about the medical-based scholarship program and how I had paid for my college and law school, she looked like she was going to throw up. Like most students, Laurie had never heard about the medical-based scholarship program when she was applying for college, and she was not at all happy to hear about it from me after the fact, especially since her medical condition was visibly more severe than mine.

It's clear to me that students can't simply rely on guidance counselors, internet searches, and word of mouth to figure out this program exists. So I hope that my new title for this program will catch on and finally help more students take advantage. With that said, let's take a look at where this program came from and how it works.

Federal Law

The medical-based scholarship program was created in 1973, under federal law, as part of the Rehabilitation Act. The Rehabilitation Act is basically a federal employment program designed to help people with medical problems find jobs. In order to further that goal, the law provides funding for people to attend college. The idea is that once someone attends college, it will be easier to find a job — thus fulfilling the purpose of the law. This is why the Rehabilitation Act works for prospective college students like you.

But since the medical-based scholarship program was created under the "Rehabilitation Act," doesn't that make it just another disability program? People frequently confuse the medical-based scholarship program for the more commonly known disability programs, but they are nothing alike.

Since the goal of the Rehabilitation Act is to get people working, it is considered an employment program, not a disability program. Whereas someone receiving disability payments is seeking financial assistance because he or she *can't* work, someone seeking funding under the medical-based scholarship program is seeking financial assistance so he or she *can* work.

But why would the government be willing to pay for people to go to college on the basis of their medical condition? The answer is pretty simple: the medical-based scholarship program is a good deal for the government. The government knows that many physically and mentally impaired people require public assistance, which must be provided at great expense to taxpayers. Therefore, the government is willing to pay for the physically and mentally impaired to attend college, get job training, or open a business. They do this because they hope these individuals will then be able to provide for themselves, without needing public assistance. People who go to college or get job training are much less likely to require public assistance, thus making the medical-based scholarship program a money saver for the government.

A college degree also tends to put people in a higher tax bracket. Essentially, the government is willing to pay for your college so that you will get a better job. The benefit to the government is that you will then pay more money in taxes. You receive a free education, and the government receives increased tax revenue from you. So from the government's perspective, money spent on the medical-based scholarship program is an investment in the tax base. This makes sense if you consider that most people will pay federal income tax for over 40 years during the course of their career. This more than compensates for the relatively small amount of money the government provides for these students to attend college for a few years.

Do I Need to Have a Serious Medical Condition?

One of the biggest misconceptions about the medical-based scholarship program is that you will only qualify if you have a really serious medical condition. This mistaken assumption is one reason most students with documented medical conditions never apply for the medical-based scholarship program — if they are fortunate enough to learn about it in the first place. After I qualified for the medical-based scholarship program, I always made it a point to discuss this program with prospective college students I would meet. I would often tell a student about the program, only to have them respond by telling me that applying for it was probably a waste of time because their medical condition "wasn't that serious."

As you are reading this, I challenge you to resist the temptation to self-evaluate your eligibility based on how serious you think your medical condition is. I frequently tell students that they may qualify for this program and they may not. But the only way to find out for sure is to submit your application. I nearly made this same mistake when I learned about the medical-based scholarship program. It's a tempting mistake to make. No one wants to waste their time filling out an application for something they think they won't qualify for. But you need to resist jumping to this conclusion. You may get it wrong and end up leaving thousands of dollars on the table in the process. And at the end of the day, this is a simple program to apply for. So even if you don't qualify, it will only take up a small amount of your time to find out for sure.

What Will the Program Pay For?

So here's the fun part. Let's imagine for a minute that you have submitted your application for the medical-based scholarship program and just found out that you qualify. What can you expect the program to pay for? If you qualify for the medical-based scholarship program, you can typically expect the program to pay for a number of expense categories. Tuition and fees are the most common. Books are also a common expense the program will pay for. In recent years, the program has also begun to pay for laptop computers. Schools often require students to have a laptop, so this is considered a necessary school supply. After tuition, fees, books, and supplies, you may also receive funds to pay for some of the incidental costs of attending college. These are referred to as "maintenance items" and can include such things as meals, housing, and transportation costs.

After graduation, and depending on your career goals, the medical-based scholarship program may also pay for you to attend graduate school. If you decide to attend graduate school, the program will provide all of the same things it provides for undergraduate students (tuition, fees, books, etc.). But this program is arguably more beneficial to graduate students since graduate school is typically more expensive.

I know this from personal experience, as the bulk of the money that I received from the program went toward my law school. My undergraduate degree was fairly cheap by comparison. However, not many students use the medical-based scholarship program to pay for graduate school. The problem with getting graduate students to apply for the medical-based scholarship program is twofold.

First, graduate students have already gone through undergrad, so they are probably familiar and comfortable with applying for student loans. Why learn something new if you already have one trick that seems to work? Second, graduate students have already accepted the fact that they are going to have some student loan debt, so what's a little more for graduate school?

Even if you already have student loan debt from attending undergrad, if you plan to attend graduate school, you should certainly consider applying for the medical-based scholarship program. It could save you a small fortune.

If you are eligible for the medical-based scholarship program, it is not a guarantee that you will receive enough money to pay for every expense associated with college. However, this is true for just about every form of financial aid. The medical-based scholarship program may not be the silver bullet for all your education expense problems, which is why I recommend exploring all of your options when it comes to the financial aid process. However, the medical-based scholarship program is one of the few free options, so I certainly encourage you to explore the free options first. It's hard to complain about free money!

Not Your Typical Scholarship

Remember how I told you that the Rehabilitation Act is technically an employment program? Well this fact creates some unusual differences from your typical college scholarship. One unique aspect of the medical-based scholarship program is that it continues to provide benefits *even after you graduate*.

For example, once you graduate, the medical-based scholarship program can assist you with finding a job in your field of study. The program may provide assistance with your résumé and with interview preparation. It may also provide you with money to purchase interview clothes. As you remember from our earlier discussion, the goal of the Rehabilitation Act is to get people working. So any employment-related expense or service that you can think of may be something the program will pay for.

Another unusual aspect of the program is that it will pay for you to get a license if one is required as a part of your career. I found this out after I had already paid $1,000 for the application for my Florida bar license. Unfortunately, the medical-based scholarship program does not reimburse you for expenses you have already paid. So, if you encounter any expense related to your education *or career*, be sure to find out whether the program will pay for it *before* you shell out the money yourself.

Another unusual aspect of the medical-based scholarship program is that college funding is just one area that it covers. Since the Rehabilitation Act is designed as an employment program, eligible applicants may also receive funding to use for job training, trade school, job placement, and even for starting a small business.

Let's face it, college isn't for everyone. I've helped many students and working adults use this program to pay for a lot of things other than college. Welding classes, bookkeeping certifications, community college, you name it and I've seen the program pay for it. Whether you want to attend college or go in another direction is something you will have to discuss when you go to apply for the medical-based scholarship program. Although this book is geared toward people who want to attend college, just be aware that other options are available, too, depending on the career path you or your loved ones want to follow.

Financial Limitations

Now let's talk about some of the not-so-good stuff. Like any other federal program, the medical-based scholarship program has its shortcomings

—the biggest of which relate to money. In some states when you apply for the medical-based scholarship program, you *may* have to complete what's referred to as a "financial needs assessment." Not all states have this requirement, but many do. In states that conduct a financial needs assessment, your financial situation can be taken into consideration to determine how much money the program will provide for your college expenses. If you are under the age of twenty-four, your parents' financial situation may also be taken into account.

Most prospective college students are under the age of twenty-four, so in states that have the financial needs assessment a high number of applicants will invariably have to deal with the implications of their parents' financial situation. If your parents are high earners, and you apply for the program in a state with a financial needs assessment, you may be entitled to little or no money through the program.

> *Disclaimer: The following paragraph is not intended to serve as tax advice for you and your family.*

In states that have a financial needs assessment, your parents' financial situation is usually not considered if your parents do not claim you as a dependent on their taxes in the year before you apply for the program. Your parents can potentially increase the amount of money you are entitled to through the program with this simple tax move. However, you should discuss the pros and cons of this to determine whether it's a good deal. If your parents are getting more money from the tax deduction than it costs for you to attend college, it might not be to their advantage to give up the deduction. However, there's a good chance your college expenses will exceed the amount of money your parents save by taking the deduction. In that case, it would make sense to forgo the deduction to be eligible for more money through the medical-based scholarship program. But again, I do not want to put myself in the position of providing tax advice to you and your family. So just be sure to have this discussion at least one year before you expect to apply for the program.

If it's too late, and your parents have already claimed you as a dependent, you should still apply for the medical-based scholarship program. Some free money is better than none. Your parents can forgo the tax deduction the following year, and then you can update your application for the medical-based scholarship program. This might result in you receiving more money through the program the following year.

In addition to the financial needs assessment, the medical-based scholarship program can also present financial limitations as a result of reduced congressional funding. Sometimes, the amount of money Congress allocates for federal programs gets reduced. This is true for every federal program out there, from prisons to national parks. When congressional funding is a problem, the medical-based scholarship program has to figure out how to serve the most students for the least amount of money. This can result in some applicants being put on a waiting list, a reduction of benefits, or limits on the number of eligible applicants. During years where congressional funding is a problem, the program implements what's called an "order of selection process," whereby the students with the most serious medical conditions receive priority.

I always encourage students to mention all the medical conditions they suffer from during the application process, because this may insulate them from the effects of reduced congressional funding. The more medical conditions you have, the higher your priority in the event the program undergoes an order of selection process due to funding problems. But don't worry: although congressional funding can be an issue, most of the time the program is well funded and operates efficiently. Just be sure to mention all your medical conditions when applying for the program, so you can hedge against any potential reductions in funding.

Why Aren't Students Aware of This Program?

One of the most common questions I get from students is, "Why haven't I heard of this program?" The typical college student first becomes aware of his or her financial aid options once they fill out a "FAFSA." FAFSA stands for Free Application for Federal Student Aid. If you're not familiar with it yet, you probably should be (fafsa.ed.gov).

ABOUT THIS PROGRAM

The FAFSA informs students in each state of their eligibility for federal student loans, grants, and work-study programs. However, the FAFSA does not inform students of their eligibility for the medical-based scholarship program. Why not?

The medical-based scholarship program is funded roughly as follows: 80 percent from the federal government and 20 percent from your state government. And while this is a federal program, it is administered by each individual state. So when students fill out a FAFSA seeking *federal* financial aid, it does not inform them of their eligibility for a *state*-administered program — despite the fact that the *federal* government provides 80 percent of the money. In short, students are not aware of the medical-based scholarship program because when they fill out a FAFSA it does not inform them of their potential eligibility.

Despite the fact that the state puts up 20 percent of the funding for the medical-based scholarship program, it still strikes me as unusual that the federal government does not inform students of their potential eligibility when they fill out a FAFSA. Each year, approximately 12 million students fill out a FAFSA in order to apply for federal student loans. The federal government knows that approximately 20 percent of those students suffer from a significant medical condition. The federal government also knows there is a federally funded program available in each state that would provide free money for these students and potentially eliminate their need for a federal loan. So why wouldn't the federal government want to inform students of their potential eligibility?

Here's my opinion: Money provided to students through federal loans is paid back to the government with interest. Money provided to students through the medical-based scholarship program is not. From a pure business perspective, would you expect the government to inform 20% of their loan customers that they could potentially get the same money for free? I don't think so.

I suspect the federal government would respond to this indictment by saying that the medical-based scholarship program, although 80 percent funded by the federal government and created and regulated by the federal government, is a state-administered program; therefore, the federal government assumes no responsibility for informing students of the program when they apply for federal student loans. Of course, this means the government receives billions of dollars in student loan repayments from people who might have qualified to get that money for free, but I'm sure it's just a coincidence.

So when students ask me why they have never heard of this program, I explain to them how the federal/state funding split operates to create a general lack of awareness. In fact, you have to dig pretty hard to find out about the medical-based scholarship program. But this fact is also what makes the medical-based scholarship program such a hidden gem. Since it's not well known, there's not much competition. There's your silver lining.

Parent's Corner

Did you know the medical-based scholarship program also applies to working adults? Typical applicants for the medical-based scholarship program are high school students and recent high school graduates. However, the program equally applies to working adults. If you are interested in seeking additional education or job training as a working adult, just follow the instructions for applying for the medical-based scholarship program described in the following chapters. The application process is the same regardless of your age. Who knows, maybe you and your child can both qualify for the program at the same time!

~ 4 ~

STARTING THE APPLICATION & DETERMINING YOUR ELIGIBILITY

1. Starting The Application

One of the worst things about applying for traditional college scholarships is the complicated application process. Students often complain about the written essay requirements, the stiff competition, the filing deadlines, and having to brag about oneself. The good news about the medical-based scholarship program is no one is going to ask you to write an essay about a time you overcame adversity or provided a valuable community service. There's also no deadline to apply, and you aren't required to brag about your accomplishments to qualify.

To begin the application process for the medical-based scholarship program, you simply need to contact your local vocational rehabilitation office ("VR office") and make an appointment to meet with a VR counselor. While this sounds incredibly simple, this is the step most prospective students never take. Making that first call is the most essential step in getting the ball rolling in the application process. There are other things that you must also do during the application process, but let's focus for a minute on what goes into making that first vital call.

How Do I Locate My Local VR Office?

There are usually dozens of VR offices in each state, but you want to make sure you get in contact with the one that serves your local area.

Finding the local VR office can sometimes be tricky, though, because different names are used to refer to this office, depending on what state you live in. In some states, it's called the Department of Rehabilitation Services; in others, it's called the Department of Human Services; in a few, it's called the Department for Workforce Development, and so on. However, all of these offices perform exactly the same function, regardless of their name, because they all operate under the same federal law — the Rehabilitation Act.

To simplify your search for the name of your local VR office, I have provided a directory in Appendix A that contains the name and contact information for the main VR office in your state. This is the headquarters or central office, governing all the VR offices in your state. If you call them, they can put you in contact with the local VR office that serves your immediate area.

I did not provide the contact information for each local VR office in every state, because the information changes so frequently it would require constant updates to the directory. The contact information and location of the main VR office in each state, on the other hand, rarely changes.

I update this directory once a year to ensure the information is accurate, but if for some reason you call the number listed in this directory and the phone number has changed, you should do an internet search to locate your local VR office. I would start by searching the terms "vocational rehabilitation office" followed by the name of your city or town. If this doesn't work, I would recommend contacting the Rehabilitation Services Administration ("RSA") in Washington, DC. This is the federal agency that governs each state's VR program.

If you have to contact this agency, just tell them you are trying to make contact with the VR office in your state and request their assistance. You can find the RSA website at rsa.ed.gov. The biggest reasons students don't take advantage of the medical-based scholarship program are that they never learn about it, or can't figure out who to call. So you need to have a clear understanding of how to locate your local VR office, regardless of what name it goes by. After you locate them, it's time to make the call.

What Do I Say When I Call?

After you find the number for your local VR office, you need to call and schedule an appointment. When you call, tell the receptionist that you would like to schedule an appointment to meet with a VR counselor. If he or she asks you why you want to make an appointment, just say that you want to discuss your eligibility for VR services on the basis of your medical condition. If you're asked what kind of services you are interested in, just say you are interested in applying for "education and training services."

It's important to speak the VR language when you make this first call. Remember earlier when I told you I created the term "medical-based scholarship program?" Occasionally, I will get an email from a student who contacted their local VR office and told them that they wanted to apply for the medical-based scholarship program, only to be told that they had the wrong number. To avoid any similar issues, remember to use the terminology that the VR office is used to hearing. So, let me repeat what I said because it is so important:

When you call, tell them you want to discuss your eligibility for "VR services." If they ask what services you are interested in applying for, tell them, "education and training services."

When Do I Call?

Unlike traditional scholarships, there is no fixed deadline when it comes to applying for the medical-based scholarship program. However, by law VR offices usually have 60-90 days after your first appointment to process your application and inform you of your eligibility. So make sure that you set up your appointment at least 90 days before your college tuition is due, because you want to finish the application process before you start your first semester of college. It's important to keep this time frame in mind when applying to colleges, because if you wait too long to schedule your appointment with the VR office, your tuition may be due before your eligibility determination is complete. In this case, you may end up having to pay for your first semester's tuition out-of-pocket or having to wait a semester to begin college.

Remember: The Medical-based scholarship program does not reimburse you for college expenses that you have already paid. So don't make the mistake of thinking VR will cut you a check after the fact just because you had already begun the application process when tuition came due. Play it safe, and make your first appointment with your local VR office at least 90 days before tuition is due. And if you are already in college and want to apply for the medical-based scholarship program, you should make your first appointment with VR at least 90 days before the next semester begins.

Some students are incredibly ambitious and want to apply a year or two before they plan to start college. While I applaud these students for being so motivated, applying really, really early is not recommended, since this gives the VR office more time to scrutinize every detail of your application, which increases the likelihood it could be denied or delayed for some reason. If the VR office knows you aren't expecting to need their services for a few years, you may end up on a waiting list, and it may prove difficult to get off the list when you actually need the money.

I advise students to apply exactly 90 days before tuition is due. No more, no less. Your application is then processed in exactly the correct time frame, without any time for additional scrutiny. And it's important to note that although the VR office legally has 60-90 days to process your application, it usually happens much sooner. On average, I would say that it usually takes approximately six weeks. But when applying to colleges, you should plan on the process taking the full 90 days so that no problems arise.

What State Do I Call?

Many students plan to attend college out-of-state, so naturally the question may arise about which state to apply in — the one you live in, or the one where you're planning to attend school. Generally speaking, you should apply at a local VR office in your home state, regardless of where you plan to attend college. If your local VR office determines that you are eligible for the medical-based scholarship program, the money can be used at an out-of-state college. Applying in a state where you don't currently live can be problematic because of residency requirements. If you qualify for the medical-based scholarship program in your home state, you may want to discuss with your VR counselor the pros and cons of applying in the state where you are attending college, once you move to that state.

2. Determining Your Eligibility

Once you have located your local VR office and scheduled an appointment, you have officially begun the application process for the medical-based scholarship program. So what's next?

At this point you need to understand what it takes to qualify. When you go to the appointment you scheduled, the VR counselor is going to determine whether you qualify for the program, so it's extremely important to know what factors he or she is going to base their decision on. Let's refer to this as the "eligibility standard."

In order to qualify for the medical-based scholarship program, the Rehabilitation Act requires applicants to have a medical condition that "impedes or has the potential to impede employment." Remember that the Rehabilitation Act is technically an employment program, so in order to qualify, your medical condition has to have some impact on your future employment.

This eligibility standard comes directly from the Rehabilitation Act itself, and all VR offices in every state are required to use it. The VR counselor you meet during your appointment is going to determine if you meet this standard by conducting a personal interview with you. We will discuss the personal interview in the next chapter, but for now let's focus on what this eligibility standard means and how it works in practice. The easiest way to demonstrate how this eligibility standard works is to use my medical condition as an example.

When I went to apply for the medical-based scholarship program, I suffered from allergies and asthma. These medical conditions had the potential to impede my employment if I were to take a job that required me to work around animals. I'm allergic to animals, so working around them would be very difficult for me. I would be constantly sneezing, itching, and coughing at work. Because allergies could potentially impede my employment as an animal worker, I met the eligibility standard for the medical-based scholarship program. Make sense? Essentially, if there is any job out there that might be difficult for someone with your medical condition to perform, there is a good chance that you will qualify for the medical-based scholarship program to pay for college.

The eligibility standard for the medical-based scholarship program requires you to demonstrate that your medical condition could negatively impact you in the employment world. So, before you begin the application process for the medical-based scholarship program, you need to think about your medical condition and exactly how the symptoms could negatively impact your employment. Understanding how your eligibility for the medical-based scholarship program is determined is crucial, because if you don't understand this process, you may unwittingly shoot yourself in the foot during the application process.

For example, during the application process, you may have to fill out a form that asks if you have any limitations in your employment. If you check the "no" box, it may be game over for your application. In this scenario, the VR counselor might determine that you don't meet the eligibility standard because you just admitted that your medical condition does not impede your employment.

This is a common mistake people make in the application process, because it's natural for people to deny questions that ask about limitations. These people may have medical conditions that could potentially create limitations in their employment, but they are psychologically conditioned to deny them. They mistakenly believe that just having a medical condition means they will qualify, but this is only one part of the equation. You have to have a medical condition, *and* that medical condition has to impede or potentially impede your employment.

When preparing for the application process, you need to ask yourself what jobs or types of work might be difficult to perform because of your medical condition. If you can come up with a few examples, you will be leaps and bounds ahead of most applicants.

What Medical Conditions Qualify?

One of the first questions I usually get from students and parents about the medical-based scholarship program is, "What medical conditions qualify?" The short answer is there is no list of medical conditions that are always guaranteed to qualify. If you've been paying attention, then you already know why this is the case.

The name of your medical condition isn't really important. What is important is whether your medical condition, whatever name it goes by, impedes or has the potential to impede your employment.

But aren't there some medical conditions that by their very nature will always impede employment? The answer to this question is yes, but if you are an applicant with one of these medical conditions, and during the application process you deny any impediments are created by your medical condition, you will not qualify. The eligibility standard is unforgiving. But the eligibility standard is also why so many students potentially qualify for the medical-based scholarship program.

If your eligibility were only determined by looking at a list of medical conditions to see if yours was on the list, many people with legitimate medical limitations might be left out of this program. But because the eligibility standard is open to interpretation, it is useful in helping a much broader group of people.

Although the name of your medical condition does not factor into the eligibility standard, I have provided a few common types of medical conditions below that I think could potentially impede employment, and, therefore, potentially qualify an applicant for the medical-based scholarship program. I only do this because many times, when I speak to a student about the medical-based scholarship program, I'll begin by asking them if they have any medical conditions. The student will frequently tell me they don't have any medical conditions, but when I tell them I qualified based on allergies, they will tell me they also suffer from allergies. So I have concluded that students need some kind of list to get an idea of what conditions could potentially qualify.

But remember, this is not an exclusive list of all qualifying medical conditions. No such list exists. These are only examples of medical conditions that I think could potentially impede employment in order to give you some idea about what the program covers. If your medical condition is not on this list, don't be discouraged from applying. In fact, if you have any medical condition whatsoever, you should apply for the medical-based scholarship program. I'm not a medical expert, so there may be many more medical conditions that could be included below.

Learning Disabilities
Attention deficit disorder (ADD); attention deficit hyperactivity disorder (ADHD); dyslexia; dyscalculia; dysgraphia; dyspraxia; dysphasia; auditory processing disorder; visual processing disorder

Musculoskeletal Disorders
Carpal tunnel syndrome; repetitive strain injury; tendonitis; tennis elbow; eye strain; back pain; shin splints; scoliosis; bunion; bone cyst; bone disease; shoulder injury; wrist injury; hand injury; neck injury; knee injury; unequal leg length; arthritis; bone deformities; sports injuries

Respiratory Impairments
Asthma; allergy; chronic bronchitis; chronic obstructive pulmonary disease (COPD); inflammatory lung disease; cystic fibrosis; emphysema; respiratory distress syndrome; tuberculosis; mesothelioma; pulmonary embolism

Mental Impairments
Bipolar disorder; depression; obsessive compulsive disorder; agoraphobia; insomnia; panic disorder; post-traumatic stress disorder; stuttering and speech disorders; social anxiety; sleep disorder; acute stress disorder; anxiety disorder; anorexia; Asperger syndrome; antisocial personality disorder; binge eating disorder; body dysmorphic disorder; autism; bulimia; hypochondria; gender identity disorder; impulse control disorder; hypomanic episode disorder

Neurological Impairments

Epilepsy; fibromyalgia; migraine; Huntington's disease; hydrocephalus; hypoxia; Lyme disease; meningitis; motor skills disorder; multiple sclerosis; muscular dystrophy; narcolepsy; Parkinson's disease; pinched nerve; pituitary disorders; restless leg syndrome; schizophrenia; shingles; sleep apnea; spina bifida; spinal cord injury; Tourette syndrome; brain injury; cerebral palsy; spinal cord conditions;

Immune System Impairments

Lupus; HIV; vasculitis; sclerosis; scleroderma; polymyositis; dermatomyositis; connective tissue disorder

Cardiovascular Impairments

Heart disease; heart failure; hypertension; arrhythmia; peripheral arterial disease; ventricular dysfunction; myocardial ischemia

Miscellaneous

- Digestive conditions: peptic ulcer; stenosis; ulcerative colitis; Crohn's disease; irritable bowel syndrome; gastrointestinal disorder
- Genito-urinary conditions: chronic nephritis; polycystic disease; bilateral hydronephrosis; renal impairments
- Hemic and lymphatic impairments: sickle cell anemia; myelofibrosis; thrombocytopenia; telangiectasia; leukemia; myeloma; anemia
- Skin conditions: burn injury; dermatitis; erythema; psoriasis; mycotic infections
- Endocrine impairments: thyroid disorders; morbid obesity; diabetes; hyperparathyroidism; hypoparathyroidism
- Vision, hearing, and speech impairments
- Hemophilia; temporomandibular joint disorder; liver disease; cancer; hemiplegia; stroke; amputation.

Parent's Corner

Be sure your child has a firm understanding of the eligibility standard before beginning the application process for the medical-based scholarship program. This will help prevent any elementary application mistakes such as admitting he or she has no potential limitations in their employment. Be sure to discuss with your child the symptoms of their medical condition and how these symptoms could negatively impact his or her future employment. This is incredibly important. The eligibility standard is the most important concept to grasp during the application process for the medical-based scholarship program. Helping your child make the connection between their medical condition and jobs or types of work that could be more difficult because of their medical condition is the single most important factor during the application process.

~ 5 ~

GETTING PREPARED FOR YOUR FIRST MEETING

Making a Good First Impression

It's probably the most overused cliché in the English language, but I'll say it here anyway: "You only get one chance to make a good first impression." In the case of your personal interview with VR, it's particularly important to make a good first impression. The VR counselor you meet with during your first appointment will most likely be the same VR counselor you are assigned for at least the next four years, and potentially longer if you plan to attend graduate school. You need to make a good first impression because from the time that you make the first appointment, the VR counselor already knows that you may be on his or her caseload for many years. So you definitely don't want your VR counselor coming away from your first meeting with a poor impression of you.

I'm not saying that your eligibility is determined by whether or not your VR counselor likes you. The law is black-and-white and applies to everyone equally. However, in the event your eligibility for the medical-based scholarship program is a close call, it really can't hurt for you to have made a good first impression on your VR counselor. Making a good first impression may be enough to help tip the balance in your favor in this situation.

Unfortunately, the opposite is also true.

The tips in this chapter are designed to help you make a good first impression and make the application process as smooth as possible. Essentially, you want to make sure your case is an easy one for the VR counselor. This means you need to be friendly, prepared, on time, and knowledgeable during your first meeting.

General Interview Tips

To make a good first impression, you need to make sure you interview well. But interviewing well can be difficult if you are a nervous wreck! It's perfectly normal to feel nervous before an interview. In fact, interviews and public speaking rank pretty high on the list of things people dread most in life. Most of the time, the source of this nervousness comes from feeling unprepared or feeling that you don't know what to expect. There's nothing worse than being asked to talk about something you don't know about or aren't really prepared to discuss. This is particularly true if you have never interviewed for something before and the whole process is new to you. So let's begin by discussing some general interview tips and practices that are good to know when going into any type of interview.

With any type of interview, you generally want to keep your body language in check. You should always refrain from excessive fidgeting, unexpected or out-of-context hand gestures, slouching, touching your face, twirling your hair, or mumbling. Poor body language can be distracting to the person conducting the interview, which means the interviewer may not focus on what you are saying.

You also want to make sure you are dressed appropriately. What qualifies as appropriate attire depends on the type of interview you are preparing for. Job interviews require you to dress professionally. However, for a personal interview with VR, you should dress "business casual." For guys, this usually means slacks and a button-down shirt. You aren't interviewing for a job, so leave the suit and tie at home. For ladies, you generally want to be fully covered and stick to neutral colors that aren't too loud. Long pants or long skirts, and tops with a high neckline, are generally safe. Both men and women should also keep jewelry, perfume/cologne, and accessories to a minimum, and avoid smoking or eating right before an interview. Smells of any type can be distracting.

You should also be sure to familiarize yourself with the location of the interview ahead of time. I know everyone has navigation in their car or on their phone these days, but I still suggest doing a dry run the day before so there aren't any surprises on the day of your interview. This will ensure you arrive on time, and you aren't frustrated because you've just spent half an hour trying to figure out where you were going and where you should park.

On the day of your appointment, you should try to arrive at least 15 minutes early. This will give you time to get settled in and be thinking about the talking points you prepared for the interview.

Before you walk in to an interview, be sure to shut off your cell phone and get rid of any chewing gum. Either one can be a source of distraction during your interview. As you walk into the office, be polite and offer a friendly greeting to everyone you engage with, from parking attendants and receptionists to the person who will conduct your interview.

Upon meeting the person who will conduct your interview, you should stand, smile, make eye contact, and offer a firm handshake as you exchange greetings. Exhibiting a positive attitude and enthusiasm are vital in any type of interview. You want to make sure that you come across as authentic, upbeat, and confident. It's perfectly OK to make small talk during an interview, but make sure you avoid any potentially divisive topics such as politics, religion, and football teams.

When your interview is over, be sure to thank the person for the interview, and say that it was a pleasure meeting him or her. You should also be sure to ask about the next step in the process, and ask for a rough estimate on when a final decision on your case will be made.

I consider the tips in this section to be the basics. If you do nothing else, at least be on time, friendly, and presentable for your first meeting. You'll be surprised at how far simple things like this can take you. Many people don't get the basics and face an uphill battle from the very start.

The Eligibility Standard Revisited

To adequately prepare for your first meeting with a VR counselor, you need to firmly grasp the purpose of the meeting. The purpose of the personal interview with VR is to determine whether you have a medical condition that impedes or has potential to impede your employment. *Remember the eligibility standard.*

Let's break the eligibility standard down into its two major components. This means during your interview you should be prepared to discuss (1) your medical condition; and (2) potential impediments to your employment. Let's take number 1 first.

You should be prepared to discuss any topic concerning your medical condition during your personal interview with VR. This may include the details of your medical condition, the symptoms, and any medication and treatments you have been prescribed. During your personal interview, be sure to mention *all* of the various symptoms you experience as a result of your medical conditions.

With many medical conditions, there is more than one symptom. Although you may be most affected by only one or two, be sure to mention all of the symptoms that affect you during your personal interview. What you consider to be a minor symptom might make the difference between qualifying and not qualifying for the medical-based scholarship program.

When describing your medical condition, assume the VR counselor has never heard of it. Taking this attitude will ensure you describe it in sufficient detail during your interview.

Of course, to sufficiently discuss your medical condition, you need to be knowledgeable about it. The best way to make sure that you are knowledgeable about your medical condition is to read up on it before your interview. Some helpful resources to find information are the National Institutes of Health (www.nih.gov) and the Centers for Disease Control (www.cdc.gov). If you visit their websites, you can perform a database search and get a wealth of information. This will include things like methods of diagnosis, symptoms, and treatments.

You should become intimately familiar with this information as it relates to your particular medical condition so you can answer and respond to any question that may arise. While you may feel like you are already knowledgeable about your medical condition, just by virtue of living with it on a daily basis, you need to be able to convey that information to someone else. The best way to ensure you can do this is to read up on it so it's fresh in your mind.

As for the second component of the eligibility standard, you need to be able to tie your medical condition to potential impediments to your employment. So as you are reading about your medical condition, think about jobs, types of work, or job functions that would be harder for someone with your medical condition to perform.

For example, if your medical condition includes back pain, it would probably be difficult for you to take a job that includes lifting heavy objects. If your medical condition causes you dizziness, it would probably be difficult for you to take a job that required you to have good balance, such as working in building construction.

These connections between your medical condition and potential limitations in your employment are important to grasp. During your personal interview, you need to make your VR counselor aware of these connections. So how do you make your VR counselor aware of the limitations your medical condition could potentially create? Here's where an example might be useful. Let's consider my medical conditions of asthma and allergies in this mock VR interview scenario.

> **VR Counselor:** "So, Mr. White, can you tell me a little about your medical conditions?"
> **Me:** "Well, I have suffered from asthma and allergies as long as I can remember."
> **VR Counselor:** "And how do these conditions affect you?"
> **Me:** "The asthma makes it difficult to breathe when I'm having an attack. And allergies cause me to have itchy, watery eyes, and difficulty in concentrating. If I am in a classroom or working around someone wearing heavy perfume, it can be incredibly difficult to stay focused and productive, where someone else may have no problem at all. If I am working in an area that is dusty, or has open windows, my allergies can

be triggered, causing me to have difficulty in concentrating. I could never work at a job where I had to be in close proximity to animals, smoke, dust, pollen, or other things that could potentially trigger my asthma or allergies."

Notice the general talking points in this mock scenario and how they work to tie my medical conditions to potential impediments to my employment. I informed the VR counselor what my medical conditions were. I described the symptoms, and I provided a real-life example of how the symptoms could negatively impact me. Then, I provided examples of types of work that would be particularly difficult for me because of my medical conditions.

This is exactly the kind of information you want to communicate to your VR counselor during your personal interview. You don't have to say it the same way I did, but the general talking points are going to be the same. You need to make it clear that your particular medical condition could potentially impact you in the employment world. If you can make this connection between your medical condition and the employment world, you will most likely meet the eligibility standard and that is the point of your first meeting with a VR counselor. Needless to say, you have a lot riding on that first meeting. So you need to practice.

The best way to practice for your personal interview is have someone quiz you. This way you are forced to think on your feet while verbalizing your thoughts. These two things are the key to any good interview.

When you practice for an interview, always try to develop general talking points as opposed to trying to memorize verbatim responses. When you memorize responses, it means you are relying on the question being asked in a very specific way. But during your interview, the question might be asked in a different way than the way you practiced answering. If you focus on knowing your general talking points, you can adapt to the question being asked regardless of how it's asked.

To practice for your interview, simply have a friend or parent ask you to describe your medical conditions, what the symptoms are like, how they affect you, and what jobs or types of work might be more difficult for you to perform because of them. These are all general talking points that may come up during your personal interview with VR. Therefore, you should be prepared to discuss them.

Practicing out loud with a friend or parent is the best way to test yourself before your personal interview. If you do poorly during your first rehearsal with friends, go back and do it again until you are comfortable that you have it right. The last thing you want, after your personal interview ends, is to drive home thinking about everything you forgot to mention and wondering whether those omissions will negatively affect your eligibility for the medical-based scholarship program.

Other Topics of Discussion

The goal of your first meeting with a VR counselor is to determine whether you meet the eligibility standard. So at a minimum, you have to be prepared to discuss anything that relates to the eligibility standard when you go in for your interview. However, other topics may also arise during your first meeting, such as your educational and career goals. These subjects are typically discussed in more detail during your second or third meeting with your VR counselor. But they may come up during your first meeting, because talking about them will give the VR counselor a general idea of who you are and what career you want to use the program to pursue.

You should freely and openly discuss your educational and career goals with your VR counselor if it comes up during your first meeting. We will discuss this issue in more detail in the following chapter, because it is an important part of the application process. For now, you just need to know that if you qualify for the program, your VR counselor will want to steer you into a career path that takes advantage of your academic strengths. So if the topic of your educational and career goals comes up during the first meeting, be sure the career goals you mention to your VR counselor are consistent with your prior academic strengths. For example, don't tell your VR counselor you want to be a computer science major if you have failed every computer class you've ever taken. This might give your VR counselor some hesitation about using VR funds to pay for your college.

The personal interview with VR will probably be the most stressful part of the application process, because it's the part where you will have to sit down and talk to a stranger about fairly personal stuff. But it's the one part of the process where you actually have some degree of influence. By your actions, you have the ability to put yourself in the best light possible to ensure that you qualify for the medical-based scholarship program. By showing up on time, being friendly, and being responsive, you will be a welcome addition to most VR counselors' caseload.

Parent's Corner

If your child suffers from a medical condition that has never been formally diagnosed, VR will usually pay for them to see a medical professional to obtain a diagnosis. However, if you have insurance and can afford for your child to see your own family physician, I would recommend that you schedule an appointment with your own doctor instead. The doctor retained by VR may be very conservative in his or her evaluation, especially in states with high application rates. The more applicants, the less money to fund the program, so doctors inclined to make conservative evaluations can potentially help the program reduce the number of eligible applicants. Although the VR office may pay for your child to get a free diagnosis, using your child's own physician for the evaluation may be more advantageous, especially if you notify your physician you are applying for a medical-based scholarship program. Most family physicians are more than happy to help. You need to begin scheduling medical appointments for undiagnosed medical conditions at least three months before you expect your child to begin the application process for the medical-based scholarship program. This will ensure you have plenty of time to attend the appointments and obtain documentation of the treatments.

~ 6 ~

YOUR SECOND MEETING

After your first meeting with VR is over, it is common for your VR counselor to ask you to provide some personal documents to assist in the evaluation process. You will be expected to bring these documents with you to the second meeting. These documents can include a variety of things, but the three most common (that you may not already have on hand) are your educational transcripts, your and your parents' tax returns, and some medical documentation of your condition.

If you want to speed up the evaluation process, you can gather these documents before your first meeting so you already have them on hand. Having these documents on hand and ready to go will also leave a good impression with your VR counselor because it makes you appear prompt and responsive. When your VR counselor requests that you provide something, always do so as soon as possible. This goes back to making a good impression. You should never procrastinate or make your VR counselor ask you repeatedly for the same thing. Making a good first impression is just the beginning — you have to keep it up!

To get your educational transcripts, you should contact your previous institutions of education and request official transcripts. Make sure you get official transcripts because your VR office may not accept unofficial transcripts. You should save these transcripts for future use. At some point in life, you may need them again. For tax records, you will need to obtain copies of your and your parents' tax returns for the previous year. If you haven't filed a tax return, and you are under the age of 24, you will probably just need a copy of your parents' tax return.

For documentation of your medical condition, you will need a letter from your doctor describing your medical condition, how long you've suffered from it, and how it was diagnosed and treated. I suggest making a written request to your doctor for this letter so you don't leave anything out. Also, it may help your doctor because he or she can refer back to your written request to make sure they have included everything in the letter that you have asked for.

At the end of this book, in Appendix B, I have provided a sample letter you can use as a template to create your written request to your doctor. In your written request, you simply need to let your doctor know that you are applying for a medical-based scholarship program, and that you need a letter about your medical condition in order to apply. The letter your doctor writes does not have to be incredibly long or detailed, but it needs to specifically state what your medical condition is, how it was diagnosed and treated, and how long you've suffered from it. It will also benefit you if your doctor will provide a statement indicating that, in his or her opinion, your medical condition has the potential to present limitations in your employment. Remember the eligibility standard.

Even if your doctor includes a statement to this affect, your VR counselor is still the final authority on determining whether your medical condition has the potential to impede your employment. But such a statement by your doctor certainly can't hurt!

Be sure to request that your doctor provide this information for each medical condition you suffer from. Once you receive the letter from your doctor, review it and make sure it addresses the things you asked him or her to address. If anything has been omitted, don't hesitate to contact your doctor and ask for revisions before you submit the letter to your VR counselor.

Your Eligibility Decision And The Written Plan

After your personal interview is over, and you have provided your VR counselor all the documents and information needed to complete your application, your VR counselor will be able to tell you whether you qualify for the medical-based scholarship program. This usually occurs within about six weeks after you provide all the documents your VR counselor will request. Once you've qualified for the program, the next step in the process is to sit down with your VR counselor and create what's referred to as your "written plan."

The written plan that you develop with your VR counselor is an outline that includes the details of your education and career goals going forward. It is somewhat like a contract. It specifies what services the program will provide and what obligations you might have to meet as a condition of receiving funding. The written plan will include details on the college that you plan to attend, the major that you plan to select, and how much money the program will provide for your tuition, books, supplies, and maintenance. It will also include an anticipated timeline for your graduation, and details on what kind of job or career you plan to pursue after college.

You and your VR counselor are both required to sign and date the written plan after it's complete. It will be periodically reviewed to monitor your progress toward accomplishing the goals set forth in it. It will also include any obligations your VR counselor may want you to uphold as a condition of receiving the money. This is an important part of the written plan, so let's discuss what kinds of obligations you might have to meet, and the potential consequences if you fail to keep up your end of the bargain.

Choosing a Major

As a condition of receiving funding under the medical-based scholarship program, you must choose a college major that is compatible with your academic strengths and that furthers your overall career goals. This means that your VR counselor will look at your old transcripts to determine whether the major you want to pursue is a good fit for you. So, in discussing the major that you plan to pursue, you should narrow your selection down to the subjects in which you tend to get the best grades.

As you may recall from the last chapter, I don't recommend you tell your VR counselor that you want to be a science major if your report cards show that you have failed every science class you have ever taken. Although you do get to select your own major, the VR counselor has to approve it before you get the scholarship money, and the best way to get approval is by majoring in a subject you tend to do well in.

This doesn't mean that you cannot change your major once you have selected it. As I said before, your written plan is periodically reviewed, and you can request changes when this happens. But any new major that you select must also be one that you can demonstrate academic strength in, and your counselor must still approve it. The rationale behind this requirement is that it reduces the risk that you will fail your courses and your college career will be over, which also reduces the risk that the scholarship money will be wasted.

This is the part of the process where your VR counselor has some discretion over your future that he or she can exercise. VR counselors are more than willing to work with you regarding what you would like to do with your life, but they also get to have their say in which direction you take. I don't consider this requirement to be a bad thing. At the end of the day, this should not really have an impact on you because you probably shouldn't major in something you aren't good at anyway!

Psychological Evaluation

Sometimes, it isn't clear to VR counselors if a student is capable of successfully pursuing a certain major even after looking at their transcripts. Therefore, counselors will occasionally ask students to submit to a psychological evaluation.

Why would such an evaluation be necessary? Let's say you have consistently gotten straight C's in every subject since you were in kindergarten. In that situation, it's not entirely clear what subject you are best at.

Let's say that during the course of developing your written plan, you tell your VR counselor you want to become a social worker when you graduate. Your VR counselor may want to know if you are capable of actually becoming a social worker before he or she approves VR funds to pay for your college experience. Thus, you might be asked to undergo a psychological evaluation to help the counselor make that determination. After the evaluation is complete, your VR counselor will get a copy of the report. If the report confirms your capability for a social work career, your VR counselor will most likely agree with your decision to major in social work.

If you are asked to undergo a psychological evaluation, you will usually have to meet with a psychologist who will conduct an interactive interview with you that is designed to determine your fitness for a certain career. To stick with our current example, if you decide you want to become a social worker, the psychological evaluation may test for your compassion for helping others. If, on the other hand, you decide you want to become an attorney, the evaluation may test your capacity for relating to two sides of an argument.

If you have to undergo a psychological evaluation, you should research the qualities necessary to pursue your chosen career. You should be sure to display those qualities during your psychological evaluation. An easy way to prepare for a psychological evaluation is to do an online search for the phrase "qualities most needed for a career in X," where X is your chosen career path. You should read up on those qualities in advance of your meeting with the psychologist, the same way you read up on your medical condition to prepare for the personal interview.

Periodic Updates

As a condition of receiving funding under the medical-based scholarship program, you will probably be required to meet with your VR counselor once or twice per semester. These meetings are simply meant to provide your VR counselor with an opportunity to speak with you about how school is going, and to allow you to provide any required updates. During these meetings, you will usually be expected to provide your VR counselor with a copy of your grades so your VR counselor can ensure you are keeping a satisfactory grade point average. In your written plan, you will typically be required to maintain at least a 2.0 grade point average. You will also be required to take a minimum number of classes per semester (usually about four classes).

Your periodic meetings with your VR counselor are meant to ensure you are keeping up your end of the written plan. You always want to make sure you show up for these meetings. If you can't make it on the scheduled day and time, be sure to call and let your VR counselor know at least 24 hours in advance.

Complying with Your Written Plan

As long as you comply with all the requirements of your written plan, you will continue to receive funding until you graduate. Once you start receiving the money, it can't be taken away from you unless you fail to comply with your obligations under the written plan. Therefore, it's incredibly important to know what's in your written plan and to keep up with your obligations. So what happens if you don't comply with your obligations under the written plan?

The typical student who falls out of compliance with their written plan can expect funding to be suspended or terminated, but not necessarily immediately. Let's say you fail to keep your grade point average above a 2.0. In that case, you will likely be placed on probationary status and given one additional semester to bring your grades up. If you don't raise your grade point average above 2.0 after one additional semester, the program may discontinue funding.

There are also circumstances under which a student may have to actually *reimburse the program* for failing to comply with the written plan. Let's say you enroll in five classes at the beginning of a semester, but after the semester begins, you drop one class, resulting in your college sending you a check. That check would have to be given to your VR counselor to reimburse the program. This money would be considered an overpayment, and you are required to give it back when this happens. If you decide you need to drop a class, this should be discussed with your VR counselor ahead of time and arrangements should be made for reimbursement of overpayments and changes to your written plan.

A student may also have to reimburse the program for using funds for an unintended purpose. Let's say you develop a written plan with your VR counselor that states you intend to become an attorney, but upon graduating from college, you don't apply to law school. You could face a situation where VR seeks reimbursement for the money provided for your undergraduate degree. This is why it is important to always know what is included in your written plan and to comply with it. If you initially created a written plan that includes plans for law school but later change your mind, you need to discuss this with your VR counselor and change your written plan before you graduate. This could help you avoid a situation where you might be asked to reimburse the program.

I have personally seen this happen to only one student, so I think it is a fairly uncommon event in the medical-based scholarship program. But you should be aware of this potential problem when you are developing your written plan. You don't want to misjudge your career path and then fail to correct it in your written plan when things change.

When Do I Receive The Funds?

After you have finished working with your VR counselor to develop your written plan, your counselor will authorize a check to be sent to your college to pay for your tuition at the beginning of each semester until you graduate, and a separate check to your college bookstore to pay for your textbooks. You may also receive a personal check to pay for some of the incidental costs of attending college (maintenance items), such as transportation, housing, and meals. Your VR counselor will also make arrangements to purchase and provide you with any necessary school supplies, such as a laptop.

You will not receive a lump sum to pay for your entire college education all at once. Your tuition is paid for at the beginning of each semester, provided that you continue to meet all of the obligations of your written plan.

I've seen plenty of students fall out of eligibility because of some failure to keep up their end of the bargain as outlined in their written plan. These students always seem surprised, and claim to have had no knowledge of what was in their written plan, even though they were required to sign and date it. Just like any contract, you should read your written plan so that you know what's expected of you. There's nothing worse than losing free money! After you start receiving funding, you have successfully completed the entire application process for the medical-based scholarship program!

Parent's Corner

So far we have only discussed what happens if your child qualifies for the medical-based scholarship program. But what happens if your child doesn't? If you feel that your child has been improperly denied eligibility, you can appeal that decision and have a neutral third party review the VR counselor's decision. This appeals process is conducted through what's known as the "Client Assistance Program" (CAP). To get the contact information for the CAP, just ask your VR office for the phone number and contact information. The CAP will obtain your child's file and review the decisions made to ensure that your child has been properly evaluated under the law. The CAP exists to ensure that mistakes regarding eligibility are corrected. If your child has been improperly denied eligibility, you want to make sure that mistake is corrected!

The possibility that your child might be denied eligibility is also why I recommend students submit a letter from their doctor during the application process. Ideally, this letter should state that in the doctor's opinion, your child's medical condition has the potential to impede their employment. If your child is denied eligibility, and you appeal your case to the CAP, the letter from your child's doctor will be included in the file the CAP reviews. This letter is powerful evidence that your child may have been improperly denied eligibility. A letter from your child's doctor may provide grounds for the CAP to reverse the decision of your child's VR counselor, thus making your child eligible for funding.

~ 7 ~

REASONABLE ACCOMMODATIONS

Now that I've walked you through the entire application process for the medical-based scholarship program, we need to discuss the topic of "reasonable accommodations." By reasonable accommodations, I'm not talking about a 3-star Holiday Inn with scratchy bath towels. A reasonable accommodation means your high school, college, or job does something for you, in order to make your medical condition easier to cope with.

For example, if your medical condition is attention deficit disorder, one of the symptoms is difficulty in maintaining focus. On test day, if you suffer from attention deficit disorder, the sound of shuffling papers or people entering and exiting the exam room may completely derail your train of thought leaving you at a disadvantage. Therefore, you may be entitled to a reasonable accommodation from your school to ease this burden.

A reasonable accommodation in this case might mean your school provides you with a private room and/or extra time to complete your exams. In fact, extra time and a private test room are probably the most common accommodations granted in educational contexts. You can request a reasonable accommodation from your high school, college, or job, whether you have qualified for the medical-based scholarship program or not. So how are these two things related?

Reasonable accommodations can serve as a beneficial precursor to applying for the medical-based scholarship program — especially if you are still in high school. So let's talk for a minute about reasonable accommodations from a high school student's perspective. If you have already graduated from high school, don't skip this section, though. There's stuff here for you too.

Reasonable accommodations and the medical-based scholarship program have many things in common as it relates to their eligibility standards. For example, if you are a high school student seeking to qualify for a reasonable accommodation, you have to have a medical condition that creates difficulty for you in the learning environment. On the other hand, to qualify for the medical-based scholarship program, you have to have a medical condition that creates difficulty for you in the employment environment. As you can see, these eligibility standards are very similar to each other.

So requesting a reasonable accommodation while you're still in high school can help you qualify for the medical-based scholarship program once you apply. When you apply for the medical-based scholarship program, you can provide documentation that shows your VR counselor that you have already been receiving reasonable accommodations for your medical condition in high school. This will show your VR counselor that you have already been determined eligible for something that has very similar requirements to the medical-based scholarship program. Prior eligibility of this kind can be a strong argument in your favor when your VR counselor makes your eligibility determination.

As with the documentation of your medical condition, you should get your high school to provide a record of accommodations they have made in writing, so you can submit it to your VR counselor as a part of your application materials. If you received accommodations in high school, you want to make sure the record of those accommodations is included in your application file. In the event you are denied eligibility for the medical-based scholarship program, you can appeal that decision through the CAP, and your record of previous accommodations in high school may help you get the denial of eligibility with VR reversed.

Many high school students I speak with want to apply for the medical-based scholarship program a few years before they graduate high school. But I always tell them to wait, that you don't want to apply too early. In the meantime, though, I tell these students that if they want to improve their chances of qualifying for the medical-based scholarship program, they should begin by seeking reasonable accommodations from their high school. It's a great way to improve your chances of qualifying for the medical-based scholarship program before you apply.

To seek a reasonable accommodation, you simply need to have a discussion with your school administrators and request that they provide you with an accommodation because of your medical condition. They may ask you to provide some medical documentation to justify your request — again, similar to the medical-based scholarship program. After you have made the request and provided any needed documentation, your school will either approve or deny your request for accommodation. But even if your request is denied, you can still show your VR counselor that you tried to get an accommodation in high school based on your medical condition, and even this may help your eligibility determination with VR, because it gives your application more credibility.

There are also other advantages to requesting reasonable accommodations while you're still in high school. If you receive extra time and a private test room to take your high school exams, it could result in you getting better grades. How many times have you taken a test and thought to yourself, "I could have gotten a perfect score if I just had more time"? Getting better grades in high school means you will be able to get into better colleges, and potentially qualify for more financial aid. Getting into better colleges also means you can pursue better jobs after graduation.

If you receive reasonable accommodations to take your high school exams, it can also help you qualify for reasonable accommodations when it's time to take the SAT. This is an incredible advantage many students with qualifying medical conditions never learn about. You can request a reasonable accommodation to take the SAT whether you have received a reasonable accommodation from your high school or not. However, to improve your chances of qualifying for a reasonable accommodation to take the SAT, you should first request an accommodation to take your regular high school exams. This will give your request more credibility, because it will appear that you have been pursuing reasonable accommodations for reasons other than just taking the SAT.

If you are interested in applying for a reasonable accommodation to take the SAT, go to collegeboard.org. This is the same website where you register to take the SAT. Just look for "Services for Students with Disabilities." This section will tell you the eligibility requirements and how to submit your request for accommodation.

If you are denied a reasonable accommodation for taking the SAT, consider registering to take the ACT instead. You can make the same request for accommodation by going to act.org and clicking on the tab that says, "Services for Examinees with Disabilities." The SAT folks may turn you down, but the ACT folks might give you the accommodation you are requesting. You can apply for college after taking either exam, but you may get a higher score on the test you took with the help of extra time and a private test room.

Reasonable accommodations can be incredibly helpful for high school students. But if you've already graduated, they are still helpful. You can request a private room and extra time for exams once you begin college or graduate school, whether you have qualified for the medical-based scholarship program or not. But if you've qualified for the medical-based scholarship program, reasonable accommodations become easier to justify. You will simply need to speak with your college administrators and let them know you are receiving funding under the Rehabilitation Act to attend college for a medical disability and you would like to discuss the need for a reasonable accommodation.

If your college administrators are reluctant to provide you with an accommodation, you can contact your VR counselor and get them involved in the conversation. Your VR counselor can contact your college administrators and facilitate the accommodation you are requesting. The fact that you are receiving funds to pay for college based on your medical condition makes it pretty difficult for your college to deny your request for reasonable accommodation based on the same medical condition.

When it comes to reasonable accommodations, just remember the key word is *reasonable*. If you can't tie your medical condition to the accommodation you're requesting, your high school or college may legitimately deny it. Basically, the accommodation you request must be a reasonable response to a problem presented by your medical condition. You can request any accommodation you'd like, but I've found a private test room and extra time for exams are the most frequent and helpful accommodations granted.

While I have never heard of a student requesting a reasonable accommodation in relation to the education curriculum itself, I can see how it would be technically possible. For example, if your medical condition involves back pain, you should be able to get a waiver for taking a required physical education course. Or if your medical condition involves a learning or speech disability, you should be able to opt out of a foreign language requirement. Essentially, I think it's possible for you raise the reasonable accommodation requirement to bypass certain classes if your medical condition creates an impediment to their completion. Again, I have never heard of a student using the reasonable accommodation requirement in this fashion, but I believe it is possible from a legal standpoint. If your school has any required class that by its very nature is problematic for you because of your medical condition, you should discuss this with your school administrators and/or VR counselor.

And finally, you should also be aware that reasonable accommodations don't stop when you graduate from college — they continue into the workplace. Once you graduate and begin working, you can request that your employer provide reasonable accommodations in response to the challenges presented by your medical condition. Employers have to comply with this requirement just like schools do. For example, if your medical condition involves a leg injury, you could request a reasonable accommodation for an office on the first floor and your employer would probably be required to provide it.

Parent's Corner

Parents are often concerned that by applying for the medical-based scholarship program, their child will suffer some kind of negative, long-term consequence, such as employers having a record of their child being "disabled." If your child qualifies for the medical-based scholarship program, employers will not have access to that information unless your child wants them to. But qualifying for the medical-based scholarship program may entitle your child to hiring preferences in certain circumstances. This is one of the benefits under the Americans with Disabilities Act (ADA) and the Rehabilitation Act. If your child wishes to apply for jobs as someone with a disability, he or she will need to request what's referred to as a "Schedule A" letter from the local VR office that provided your child with client services. When your child applies for a job, he or she can submit this letter as a part of the application process. This letter informs the employer that your child is eligible for hire under the ADA and Rehabilitation Act but does not disclose any medical information about your child. Once your child graduates from college, you should request a Schedule A letter to keep for your records. Your child may decide to use this letter during their future job searches.

~ 8 ~
CONCLUSION

Colleges and student loan providers look at you as a small fish to be gobbled up as they saddle you with a lifetime of debt repayments. The game is rigged against you, and you have to learn to fight back. The cost of a college degree has increased over 1,100% since the 1970s. Meanwhile, I seriously doubt the cost of putting students in a room to listen to a professor give a lecture has increased by that much. Nevertheless, as a student, these cost increases get passed on to you. That is, unless you learn to navigate the labyrinth of loopholes and discounts that the financial-aid process has to offer.

The medical-based scholarship program provides incredible benefits to those students fortunate enough to discover it. Unfortunately, most students never become aware of this program when deciding how to pay for college. But learning about this program is only half the battle. In order to benefit from it, you have to put in some effort and make things happen.

Traits of a Successful Applicant: Ambition

Ambition is the first step toward success in any endeavor. Ambitious people always make the most of the opportunities afforded them and where no opportunity exists, they learn to create their own. Ambitious people dream of success, and they take steps to make those dreams come true. Ambitious people are hard-working, and they are always looking for a way to move on to the next step of accomplishing their goals.

By contrast, people who aren't ambitious usually dream of getting out of work or just getting by. But this dream often has the tendency of backfiring. People who aren't ambitious usually end up working much harder than ambitious people — and, ironically, achieving much less.

For example, starting the application for the medical-based scholarship program only requires a five-minute phone call, but many students (and unfortunately their parents) often tell me things like, "My medical condition isn't that serious, so applying is probably a waste of time." I've seen these same students go on to spend an entire day applying for a student loan. They can't seem to muster up the effort to make a five-minute phone call, and as a result, they spend the next 20–30 years working to repay a student loan.

Persistence

Persistence, by definition, means your ambition has staying power. You get up every time you get knocked down. You rise to meet every new obstacle. It is said that Thomas Edison developed thousands of failed prototypes for the lightbulb before finally designing the version we recognize today. After failing several times, many concluded that Edison's whole endeavor was a failure. But Edison replied, "I've not failed; I've just found 10,000 ways that won't work."

This story embodies the meaning of persistence, and it has relevance to the medical-based scholarship program. It's not enough for you to make a five-minute phone call to your local VR office. You also have to schedule the appointment. You then have to show up to the appointment. You also have to be prepared when you get there.

Many students I've tried to assist in the medical-based scholarship program start the process, and for whatever reason, don't complete it. Some of them call to schedule the appointment and the receptionist tells them they might not qualify, so they withdraw their application before a final determination is made. Some of them make an appointment, but never show up. Some of them qualify, but don't keep up with the requirements in their written plan. These students are not persistent.

It's easy to spot people who aren't persistent. They always seem to have goals, but never seem to take more than one or two steps toward achieving them. When you apply for the medical-based scholarship program, make sure you are persistent. Make sure you finish each step of the process. If you don't, the student loan bullies will be eagerly waiting to catch you when you fall.

Fearlessness

To be *fearless* means you are capable of taking action even though there is a possibility you may fail. Fearless people do not run from the possibility of rejection, they have the courage to fail, and they have the ability to recover when they do fail. If you are afraid to fail, then you are also afraid to succeed.

Many students I have assisted with the medical-based scholarship program express excitement upon learning about the program, but when I tell them they have to meet with a VR counselor for a personal interview, they decide they aren't interested in applying. These students dread the personal interview so much they would rather take out a student loan to pay for college. In essence, they are paralyzed by their fear and can't work through it. Fear should never be a justification for inaction. Sure, you might not qualify for the medical-based scholarship program, but if you're too afraid to even apply, you will never know.

Recap Of What You Learned

In this book, I told you everything you need to know about the medical-based scholarship program — beginning with the most important part of all, which is how to begin the application process. Use the bullet points below as a checklist to make sure that you have done everything in your power to give yourself the best chance of qualifying for the medical-based scholarship program.

I hope that this book saves you a ton of money on college expenses, and I wish you the best of luck in your future endeavors. Although I can provide you the information that you need to apply for this program, only *you* can make it happen. So, put aside any hesitation and make that call to your local VR office! You won't regret it. And remember: You can't qualify if you don't apply!

- If you are under the age of 24, speak with your parents about the pros and cons of not claiming you as a dependent on their taxes the year before you start the application process for the medical-based scholarship program.
- To begin the application process, you simply need to contact your local VR office and schedule an appointment to meet with a VR counselor.
- I have provided a directory in Appendix A that contains the name and contact information for the main VR office in your state. Call this office and request to be put you in contact with the local VR office that serves your immediate area.
- After you find the number of your local VR office, you need to call and schedule an appointment. When you call, simply tell the receptionist that you would like to schedule an appointment to meet with a VR counselor. If the receptionist asks you why you want to make an appointment, just say that you want to discuss your eligibility for VR services on the basis of your medical condition. If the receptionist asks you what kind of services you are interested in, just say you are interested in applying for "education and training services."
- Make sure that you set up your appointment with VR at least 90 days before your college tuition is due.
- You should apply at a local VR office in your home state regardless of where you plan to attend college.
- Remember that the eligibility standard requires applicants to have a medical condition that "impedes or has the potential to impede employment."
- Before you begin the application process for the medical-based scholarship program, you need to think hard about your medical condition and how the symptoms could negatively impact your employment.

- Make a good first impression during your personal interview with VR.
- During your personal interview, you should be prepared to discuss any topic concerning your medical condition. This includes being prepared to describe the details of your medical condition, the symptoms, and any medication and treatments you have been prescribed. Be sure to mention all of the various symptoms you experience as a result of all of your medical conditions.
- During your personal interview, be able to list some jobs, types of work, or job functions that would be harder for someone with your medical condition to perform.
- Obtain your education transcripts, your and your parents' tax returns, and a letter from your doctor describing your medical condition.
- For documentation of your medical condition, you will need to send a written request to your doctor asking him or her to provide a letter describing your medical condition, how long you've suffered from it, and how it was diagnosed and treated. (See Appendix B for an example of a written request asking your doctor for this information).

Parent's Corner

With a little effort, your child's medical condition can form the basis of their entire education and career strategy. I call this strategy, "the medical loophole strategy." The medical loophole strategy is a multi-tiered approach that begins in high school. The first tier involves your child getting reasonable accommodations to take their regular high school exams and their SAT or ACT. The next tier involves your child applying for the medical-based scholarship program to pay for college expenses and avoid debt. The third tier involves your child using their record of eligibility for VR services to obtain reasonable accommodations to take their college exams. The final tier involves your child using their Schedule A letter from VR to gain hiring preference for jobs after they graduate. If you can help your child begin — and stick with — this long-term strategy, they can successfully leverage their medical condition to obtain a number of advantages as they pursue their education and career goals.

~ APPENDIX A ~

DIRECTORY OF VOCATIONAL REHABILITATION OFFICES

Locate your state in the directory below. When you call the number, ask to be put in touch with the VR office in your local area. When you contact your local VR office, tell the receptionist that you'd like to schedule an appointment with a VR counselor to determine your eligibility for VR services based on your medical condition. If the receptionist asks what kind of VR services you are interested in, say "education and training services."

Alabama

Alabama Dept. of Rehabilitation Services
602 S. Lawrence St.
Montgomery, AL 36104
Telephone: (800) 441-7607
www.rehab.alabama.gov

Alaska

Alaska Dept. of Labor and Workforce Development, Division of Rehabilitation Services
1111 W. 8th Street, Ste. 210
Juneau, AK 99801-1894
Telephone: (800) 478-2815
www.labor.state.ak.us
Note: click on vocational rehabilitation division

Arizona
Arizona Rehabilitation Services Administration
3221 N. 16th St., Suite 200
Phoenix, AZ 85016-7159
Telephone: (602) 266-9206
www.des.az.gov
Note: click on vocational rehabilitation

Arkansas
Arkansas Dept. of Career Education
3 Capitol Mall
Little Rock, AR 72201
Telephone: (501) 682-1500
http://ace.arkansas.gov/arRehabServices/

California
California Dept. of Rehabilitation
721 Capitol Mall
Sacramento, CA 95814
Telephone: (800) 952-5544
www.rehab.cahwnet.gov/Vocational-Rehabilitation.html

Colorado
Colorado Division of Vocational Rehabilitation
1575 Sherman St., 4th Floor
Denver, CO 80203
Telephone: (303) 866-4150
www.dvrcolorado.com

Connecticut
Connecticut Dept. of Rehabilitation Services
55 Farmington Ave. 12th Floor
Hartford, CT 06105
Telephone: (800) 537-2549
www.ct.gov/brs/

Delaware

Delaware Dept. of Labor, Division of Vocational Rehabilitation
Blue Hen Corporate Center
655 South Bay Road, Ste 2H
Dover, DE 19901
Telephone: (302) 739-5478
http://dvr.delawareworks.com

Florida

Florida Dept. of Education, Division of Vocational Rehabilitation
4070 Esplanade Way
Tallahassee, FL 32399-7016
Telephone: (800) 245-3399
www.rehabworks.org

Georgia

Georgia Vocational Rehabilitation Agency
1718 Peachtree Street NW, Ste. 376-S
Atlanta, GA 30309
Telephone: (404) 206-6000
www.gvra.georgia.gov

Hawaii

Hawaii Dept. of Human Services, Division of Vocational Rehabilitation
1390 Miller St., Room 209
Honolulu, HI 96813
Telephone: (855) 643-1643
http://humanservices.hawaii.gov/

Idaho

Idaho State Board of Education, Division of Vocational Rehabilitation
650 W. State St., Room 150
Boise, ID 83720
Telephone: (208) 334-3390
www.vr.idaho.gov

Illinois
Illinois Dept. of Human Services, Division of Vocational Rehabilitation
401 South Clinton St.
Chicago, IL 60607
Telephone: (800) 843-6154
www.dhs.state.il.us

Indiana
Indiana Family and Social Services Administration, Division of Disability and Rehabilitative Services
402 W. Washington St., #W451
PO Box 7083 MS26
Indianapolis, IN 46207-7083
Telephone: (800) 545-7763
www.in.gov/fssa/ddrs/2636.htm/

Iowa
Iowa Vocational Rehabilitation Services
510 East 12th St.
Des Moines, IA 50319-0240
Telephone: (800) 532-1486
www.ivrs.iowa.gov

Kansas
Kansas Dept. for Children and Families, Rehabilitation Services
555 S. Kansas Ave.
Topeka, KS 66603
Telephone: (785) 368-7471
www.dcf.ks.gov
Note: Under the Rehabilitation Services tab, click on "Employment Services."

Kentucky
Kentucky Office of Vocational Rehabilitation
275 East Main St.
Mail Drop 2EK
Frankfort, KY 40621
Telephone: (800) 372-7172
http://kcc.ky.gov/Vocational-Rehabilitation/

Louisiana

Louisiana Workforce Commission, Vocational Rehabilitation Program
950 N. 22nd St.
PO Box 91297
Baton Rouge, LA 70821-9297
Telephone: (800)-737-2958
www.laworks.net
Note: Click on the Work-Force Development tab.
Then click the Louisiana Rehabilitation Services tab.
Then click the Vocational Rehabilitation Program tab.

Maine

Maine Dept. of Labor, Division of Vocational Rehabilitation
45 Commerce Drive
Augusta, ME 04333
Telephone: (800) 698-4440
www.maine.gov/rehab/

Maryland

Maryland State Dept. of Education, Division of Vocational Rehabilitation
2301 Argonne Dr.
Baltimore, MD 21218
Telephone: (888) 554-0334
www.dors.state.md.us/DORS/

Massachusetts

Massachusetts Rehabilitation Commission, Vocational Rehabilitation Program
600 Washington Street
Boston, MA 02111
Telephone: (617) 727-5550
www.mass.gov
Note: Doing a Google search for "Massachusetts Vocational Rehabilitation" will take you to the landing page much more easily than navigating the above website.

Michigan

Michigan Dept. of Health and Human Services, Michigan Rehabilitation Services

235 South Grand Ave. Ste. 414
Lansing, MI 48909
Telephone: (800) 605-6722
www.michigan.gov/mdhhs/
Note: Click on the Adult and Children's Services tab.
Then click on the MI Rehabilitation Services tab.

Minnesota

Minnesota Dept. of Employment and Economic Development, Vocational Rehabilitation Services

332 Minnesota St. Suite E-200
Saint Paul, MN 55101-1351
Telephone: (651) 259-7345
http://mn.gov/deed/job-seekers/disabilities
Note: Click on the Counseling and Training tab.
Then click on the Apply tab.

Mississippi

Mississippi Dept. of Rehabilitation Services

1281 Highway 51
Madison, MS 39110
Telephone: (800) 443-1000
www.mdrs.state.ms.us

Missouri

Missouri Dept. of Elementary and Secondary Education, Vocational Rehabilitation

3024 DuPont Circle
Jefferson City, MO 65109
Telephone: (877) 222-8963
http://dese.mo.gov/vr/vocrehab.htm/

Montana

Montana Dept. of Public Health and Human Services, Vocational Rehabilitation and Blind Services
111 N. Last Chance Gulch, Suite 4C
PO Box 4210
Helena, MT 59604-4210
Telephone: (877) 296-1197
www.dphhs.mt.gov/detd/vocrehab/

Nebraska

Nebraska Dept. of Education, Nebraska Vocational Rehabilitation
3901 N. 27th St. Ste. 6
Lincoln, NE 68521
Telephone: (877) 637-3422
www.vr.ne.us

Nevada

Nevada Dept. of Employment, Training & Rehabilitation, Bureau of Vocational Rehabilitation
1370 S. Curry St.
Carson City, NV 89703
Telephone: (775) 684-4040
http://detr.state.nv.us/
Note: Click on the Rehabilitation Division tab.

New Hampshire

New Hampshire Dept. of Education, New Hampshire Vocational Rehabilitation
101 Pleasant St.
Concord, NH 03301-3494
Telephone: (603) 271-3494
www.education.nh.gov/career/vocational/

New Jersey

New Jersey Dept. of Human Services, Division of Vocational Rehabilitation Services
1 John Fitch Way #10
Trenton NJ, 08611
Telephone: (609) 292-9339 or (609) 292-5987
http://careerconnections.nj.gov/careerconnections/
Note: Click on the Plan tab. Then click on the Vocational Rehabilitation tab.

New Mexico

New Mexico Public Education Dept., Division of Vocational Rehabilitation
435 St. Michael's Drive
Santa Fe, NM 87505
Telephone: (800) 224-7005
www.dvr.state.nm.us/

New York

New York State Education Dept., Adult Career and Continuing Education Services — Vocational Rehabilitation
80 Wolf Rd. Ste. 200 2nd Floor
Albany, NY 12205
Telephone: (800) 272-5448
www.nysed.gov/
Note: Click on the Program Offices tab. Then click on the Vocational Rehabilitation tab.

North Carolina

North Carolina Dept. of Health and Human Services, Vocational Rehabilitation Services
2801 Mail Service Center
Raleigh, NC 27699-2801
Telephone: (800) 689-9090
www.ncdhhs.gov/dvrs/

North Dakota

North Dakota Dept. of Human Services, Division of Vocational Rehabilitation

1237 W. Divide Ave., Suite 1B
Bismarck, ND 58501-1208
Telephone: (800) 755-2745
www.nd.gov/dhs/dvr/

Ohio

Ohio Bureau of Vocational Rehabilitation

150 E. Campus View Blvd.
Columbus, OH 43235-4604
Telephone: (800) 282-4536
www.ood.ohio.gov/Core-Services/BVR/

Oklahoma

Oklahoma Dept. of Rehabilitation Services

3535 N.W. 58th St., Suite 500
Oklahoma City, OK 73112
Telephone: (800) 845-8476
http://okrehab.org/

Oregon

Oregon Dept. of Human Services, Vocational Rehabilitation

500 Summer St., NE E-87
Salem, OR 97301
Telephone: (877) 277-0513
www.oregon.gov/DHS/employment/vr/

Pennsylvania

Pennsylvania Dept. of Labor, Office of Vocational Rehabilitation

1521 N. 6th St.
Harrisburg, PA 17102
Telephone: (717) 787-5244
www.dli.state.pa.us/ovr/

Rhode Island

Rhode Island Dept. of Human Services, Office of Rehabilitation Services
40 Fountain St.
Providence, RI 02903
Telephone: (401) 421-7005
www.ors.ri.gov

South Carolina

South Carolina Vocational Rehabilitation Dept.
1410 Boston Ave. West
PO Box 15
Columbia, SC 29171
Telephone: (800) 832-7526
http://scvrd.net/

South Dakota

South Dakota Dept. of Human Services, Division of Rehabilitation Services
3800 E. Hwy 34
c/o 500 E. Capital Ave.
Pierre, SD 57501
Telephone: (605) 773-3318
http://dhs.sd.gov/drs/vocrehab/vr.aspx/

Tennessee

Tennessee Dept. of Human Services, Division of Rehabilitation Services
400 Deaderick St., 2nd Floor
Nashville, TN 37243-1403
Telephone: (615) 313-4891
www.tennessee.gov/humanservices/topic/vocational-rehabilitation/

Texas

Texas Dept. of Assistive and Rehabilitative Services
4800 North Lamar Blvd.
Austin, TX 78756
Telephone: (800)-628-5115
www.dars.state.tx.us

APPENDIX A: DIRECTORY OF VOCATIONAL REHABILITATION OFFICES

Utah

Utah State Office of Rehabilitation
1595 W. 500 S
PO Box 144200
Salt Lake City, UT 84104
Telephone: (801) 887-9500
www.usor.utah.gov
Note: Click on Vocational Rehabilitation.

Vermont

Vermont Agency of Human Services, Division of Vocational Rehabilitation
HC 2 South, 280 State Drive
Waterbury, VT 05671-2040
Telephone: (866) 879-6757
http://vocrehab.vermont.gov

Virginia

Virginia Dept. for Aging and Rehabilitative Services
8004 Franklin Farms Dr.
Henrico, VA 23229-5019
Telephone: (800) 552-5019
www.vadrs.org

Washington

Washington State Dept. of Social and Health Services, Division of Vocational Rehabilitation
4565 7th Ave. SE
Lacey, WA 98503
Telephone: (800) 637-5627
www.dshs.wa.gov/dvr/

West Virginia

West Virginia Dept. of Education and the Arts, Division of Rehabilitation Services
107 Capitol St.
Charleston, WV 25301-2609
Telephone: (800) 642-8207
www.wvdrs.org

Wisconsin

Wisconsin Dept. of Workforce Development, Division of Vocational Rehabilitation
201 East Washington Avenue
PO Box 7852
Madison, WI 53707
Telephone: (800) 442-3477
http://dwd.wisconsin.gov

Wyoming

Wyoming Dept. of Workforce Services, Vocational Rehabilitation Division
614 South Greeley Highway
Cheyenne, WY 82002
Telephone: (307) 777-8650
http://wyomingworkforce.org

APPENDIX B
SAMPLE LETTER TO YOUR DOCTOR

Dear Dr. Smith,

I am in the process of applying for a medical-based scholarship program to help pay for my college expenses. As part of the application, I need to submit a written statement from my treating physician regarding my medical conditions of (_____) and (_____). I ask that you provide, at your convenience, a written statement that I can submit as a part of my application. The statement that you provide should address the following points:

1) Please describe the nature and symptoms of my medical conditions of (_____) and (_____).
2) Please describe any limitations on lifestyle or activities potentially created by my medical conditions.
3) Please describe how my medical conditions were diagnosed and treated.
4) I am more likely to qualify for the medical-based scholarship program if my medical conditions have the "potential to impede my employment." If you conclude that my medical conditions do have the potential to impede my employment, please include a statement to that effect in the letter you provide. If you do not believe my medical conditions have the potential to impede my employment, please refrain from including this opinion in your letter, so it will not hurt my chances of qualifying for the medical-based scholarship program.

Once you have completed the letter, please feel free to mail it to the address below, or contact me so I can pick it up at your office. If you have any additional questions about the letter, please call me at the number below. I hope to complete my application for the medical-based scholarship program within the next (_____) weeks, so if possible, please complete this letter on my behalf by MM/DD/YYYY. This will allow me to complete my application in a timely fashion. I thank you for your assistance.

Yours truly,

Steven Student
123 Cherry Street
Alexandria, VA 22314
Phone: (555) 555-5555

~ APPENDIX C ~

FREQUENTLY ASKED QUESTIONS

I receive a variety of questions from students about the medical-based scholarship program. These questions come from students at all phases of the process — from those just starting the process, those in the middle of the process, and from students who have already graduated and have decided they want to pursue additional education. Because this book is geared toward new applicants, I have tried to include more questions relating to issues that pop up at the beginning of the application process. I hope these help you.

Q: Can I get in trouble for faking medical symptoms to apply for a medical-based scholarship? It seems like some medical conditions would be really easy to fake.
A: I get this question from a student at least once a year. Students recognize the fact that there are medical conditions for which there are no objective medical tests (i.e., depression, anxiety, etc.). This is immoral at best and illegal at worst. I can't give anyone legal advice, but, generally speaking, if you don't have a medical condition, don't fake one. These programs only have so much money to go around, and if you decide to fake a medical condition in order to receive money, you are taking the money away from someone who genuinely needs it and legitimately qualifies for it.

Q: Is my local VR office affiliated with my college or university?
A: No. Your local VR office is not affiliated with your college. It is an independent entity. It is often located in the same building or office as other social services or disability offices in your area. Every now and then, I get a question from a student who has gone to the financial aid office and has asked to speak with a VR counselor only to be met with a confused response.

Q: My medical issue is a recent development. Am I eligible?
A: You must have suffered from your medical condition for at least six months to be eligible for the medical-based scholarship program, but even undiagnosed medical problems can qualify for the medical-based scholarship program. Even if your medical condition is a recent development, I would still encourage you to apply for the medical-based scholarship program.

Q: Did you incur any student loan debt during college and law school?
A: Yes, I did. But all of my student loan debt was accrued during law school. I earned my undergraduate degree debt-free thanks to the medical-based scholarship program, but during law school, I accumulated a small amount of college debt, because the program did not cover the full extent of my out-of-state tuition during my first year of law school. I also needed some extra money for living expenses.

Q: Does my age affect my eligibility for the medical-based scholarship program?
A: No. Although having an extensive work history may make it harder to qualify for certain services, it is not an automatic bar to eligibility. I would still encourage you to apply, regardless of your age. The nature of the Rehabilitation Act is the reason that your age may play a role in the services that you may qualify for. Remember that the goal of the Rehabilitation Act is to get people with medical conditions into the workforce. If you have a long work history, you have already demonstrated you have the ability to retain gainful employment. Therefore, you may qualify for the medical-based scholarship program, but it might only

cover additional job training, job certifications, and so on. However, it may also cover college, depending on your particular situation. The oldest person I have seen qualify for college was in his late forties.

Q: I am still in high school. When can I apply for the program?
A: You can apply in most states when you turn 16. However, I would encourage you to begin the application process 90 days before you plan to attend college. Applying a year before you plan to attend college is not recommended because it may cause your application to be overly scrutinized. Because of the length of time the VR counselors have to process your application, it could cause difficulty in the application process. In the meantime, consider requesting reasonable accommodations from your high school.

Q: I have a very serious medical condition. Am I required to meet with a VR counselor?
A: Yes. Even if your medical condition is very serious, you will still need to be evaluated by a VR counselor who will make the ultimate decision on your eligibility. When I get this question from students, it usually means that they really hate the idea of having to meet with a stranger and talk about their medical condition, and they would rather just send in their medical documentation. The personal interview is nothing to fear. This fear can be conquered by being prepared and knowing what to expect.

Q: I have already graduated from college. Can I still qualify for the medical-based scholarship program to go back to school?
A: Yes. In many respects, the medical-based scholarship program is more advantageous if you have already graduated because you may be over the age of twenty-four and won't have to worry about your parents' financial situation in any financial needs assessment. I have assisted many college graduates in qualifying for the medical-based scholarship program to pursue an advanced degree. When using the medical-based scholarship program to pay for graduate school, students often qualify for additional money that is not available for undergraduate studies.

Q: I called to make an appointment with my local VR office, and the receptionist told me I probably wouldn't qualify. Should I even bother continuing with the application process?
A: Yes. Again, you can't qualify if you don't apply. I always encourage students to go through the entire application process from start to finish until they are given an official determination letter. You cannot rely on an offhand comment from a receptionist to determine your eligibility. The only way that you can be 100 percent certain of your eligibility is to see the entire process through to the end.

Q: If I am denied eligibility in one state, can I apply in another state?
A: Yes. However, you may need to be living in the other state when you apply, due to residency requirements.

Q: It's been a while since I've heard from VR after I submitted my application. Should I follow up with them?
A: Yes. VR is required to process your application within 90 days, but everyone makes mistakes. If you haven't heard back from VR after submitting your application, you should certainly follow up with them.

Q: Are there any traditional scholarships students can apply for based on their medical conditions?
A: Yes. These scholarships tend to be specific to certain medical conditions. Below are a few resources you can explore to learn more.

- General Disability Scholarship Information: **www.disabled-world.com**
- Foundation for Science and Disability Science Student Grant Fund: **www.stemd.org**
- Incight Scholarship: **www.incighteducation..org/scholarship**
- Medical Goods: **www.medicalgoods.com/disability-scholarships/**
- Paul G. Hearne Leadership Award: **www.aapd.com/what-powers-us/leadership-awards/**

- AG Bell Financial Aid and Scholarship Program, Alexander Graham Bell Association for the Deaf and Hard of Hearing: **www.listeningandspokenlanguage.org**
- Hard of Hearing and Deaf Scholarship, Sertoma International: **www.sertoma.org**
- Minnie Pearl Scholarship Program, Hearing Bridges: **www.hearingbridges.org/scholarships**
- Visual Impairments, ACB Scholarship, American Council of the Blind: **www.acb.org**
- Physical Mobility Impairments: **www.1800wheelchair.com/scholarships**
- AmeriGlide Achievers Scholarship: **www.ameriglide.com/scholarship**
- National MS Society Scholarship Program, National Multiple Sclerosis Society: **www.nationalmssociety.org**
- Spina Bifida Association of America: **www.spinabifidaassociation.org**
- Hemophilia Federation of America: **www.hemophiliafed.org**
- Immune Deficiency Foundation: **www.primaryimmune.org**
- Ulman Cancer Fund for Young Adults: **www.ulmanfund.org**
- Anne Ford and Allegra Ford Scholarship, National Center for Learning Disabilities: **www.ncld.org**
- Hydrocephalus Association: **www.hydroassoc.org**
- Mental Health, Lilly Reintegration Scholarship: **www.reintegration.com**
- Scholarships for Disabled Veterans: **www.afcea.org**

ABOUT THE AUTHOR

Jason White used the medical-based scholarship program described in *The Medical Loophole* to pay for his college and law school. Jason has been helping students apply for the medical-based scholarship program since 1999. Jason is also a member of the Association on Higher Education and Disability (AHEAD).

Jason is currently a U.S. Department of Justice attorney who represents the Federal Bureau of Prisons. Jason is a former assistant attorney general for the state of Florida. Jason is also a former prosecutor for the Florida Department of Business. Jason is a graduate from the Florida State University College of Law and East Tennessee State University.

Jason is an avid marksman and outdoors enthusiast who once participated in the History Channel series *Top Shot*, and also enjoys traveling and kickboxing.

Made in the USA
Monee, IL
27 March 2023